TREATMENT OF THE ALCOHOL-ABUSING OFFENDER

TREATMENT OF THE ALCOHOL-ABUSING OFFENDER

By

ROBERT R. ROSS, Ph.D.

Professor, Department of Criminology
University of Ottawa
Ottawa, Ontario, Canada

and

LYNN O. LIGHTFOOT, Ph.D., Psych.

Director, Addiction Research Foundation, Kingston
Assistant Professor, Department of Psychology
Queen's University
Kingston, Ontario, Canada

CHARLES C THOMAS • PUBLISHER

Springfield • Illinois • U.S.A.

Published and Distributed Throughout the World by

CHARLES C THOMAS • PUBLISHER
2600 South First Street
Springfield, Illinois 62717

ISBN 0-398-05090-2

Library of Congress Catalog Card Number: 84-16298

With THOMAS BOOKS *careful attention is given to all details of manufacturing and design. It is the Publisher's desire to present books that are satisfactory as to their physical qualities and artistic possibilities and appropriate for their particular use.* THOMAS BOOKS *will be true to those laws of quality that assure a good name and good will.*

Printed in the United States of America
Q-R-3

Library of Congress Cataloging in Publication Data

Ross, Robert R., 1933 –
Treatment of the alcohol-abusing offender.

Bibliography: p.
Includes index.
1. Alcoholism and crime – United States.
2. Rehabilitation of criminals – United States.
3. Alcoholism – Treatment – United States.
I. Lightfoot, Lynn O. II. Title.
HV5053.R67 1985 365'.66 84-16298
ISBN 0-398-05090-2

ABOUT THE AUTHORS

ROBERT R. ROSS

BOB Ross is Professor of Criminology, University of Ottawa. He received the Ph.D. in Psychology from the University of Toronto. Dr. Ross has been Lecturer, Wilfred Laurier University; Associate Professor of Clinical Psychology, University of Waterloo; Research Associate, Human Justice Program, University of Regina; and Honorary Research Associate, Faculty of Law, University of Edinburgh. His experience in criminal justice includes more than ten years as a clinical psychologist in a wide variety of correctional institutions for juveniles and adults and twelve years as a Chief Psychologist for the Ontario Government's Ministry of Correctional Services. He has also been a faculty member for the Ontario Department of Education's programs for special education teachers, and a Consultant to the Department of Educational Television. Dr. Ross's publications include articles in professional journals in psychology, criminology and corrections, chapters in fourteen books on criminology, corrections and behavior modification, and four books: *SELF-MUTILATION* (with H.B. McKay), D.C. Heath Co., 1979; *EFFECTIVE CORRECTIONAL TREATMENT* (with P. Gendreau), Butterworths, 1980; *PRISON GUARD/CORRECTIONAL OFFICER,* Butterworths Co., 1981; and *THINKING STRAIGHT: THE COGNITIVE MODEL OF CRIME & DELINQUENCY PREVENTION & REHABILITATION* (with E. Fabiano), Institute of Social Sciences & Arts, 1985 (in press).

LYNN O. LIGHTFOOT

Lynn Lightfoot is Director, Addiction Research Foundation, Kingston, Ontario, and Assistant Professor, Department of psychology, Queen's University. She received her Ph.D. in Psychology from the University of Waterloo. She has been Research Director of the Treatment Program Development Research Project, Queen's University, and Community Consultant, Addiction Research Foundation. Her Research interests include conditioning and behavioral tolerance in social drinkers, the effects of alcohol on deviant sexual arousal, and treatment outcome research. Currently she is principal Investigator of a Correctional Services, Canada project to develop alcohol treatment programs in federal penitentiaries.

ACKNOWLEDGEMENTS

WE acknowledge the support of the Psychological Services Division, Offender Programs Branch, The Correctional Service of Canada which funded the senior author in a research project which entailed a critical review of the literature on the treatment of alcohol-abusing offenders. A report on that project was submitted in June 1982: *Alcohol Abuse Treatment in Corrections: Programs and Results.* Copyright of the project report is held by the Correctional Service of Canada. We are pleased that permission has been granted to include, as part of this book, an edited version of the project report. The encouragement of G. Pinder and R. Watkins in this research is appreciated.

We appreciate the advice of Dr. Paul Gendreau, Regional Psychologist, Ontario Ministry of Correctional Services, who served as research associate to the project. We are grateful to Jamie D. Shortt, Classification Officer, Ontario Ministry of Correctional Services. As a research assistant to the project, Jamie conducted a search of the literature on alcohol treatment in corrections. We also appreciate the assistance of Bambi D. Ross in conducting additional literature searches, preparing bibliographies, indexing, and proofreading for the project and for the book. We appreciate Roslynn Ross's suggestions on matters of style and denotation.

The views expressed in this book are those of the authors and do not necessarily reflect the views of the Ministry of the Solicitor General of Canada or the Addiction Research Foundation.

Some of the research reported in this book was conducted while the senior author was Honorary Research Associate, Faculty of Law, University of Edinburgh.

CONTENTS

TREATMENT OF THE ALCOHOL-ABUSING OFFENDER

CHAPTER 1

INTRODUCTION

IT has long been recognized that there is a link between alcohol use and criminal behavior. Alcohol has been found to be associated with the full range of criminal acts. It is implicated not only in breaches of liquor laws or traffic offences, but also in crimes of violence including assault, rape, and homicide.

A major proportion of the correctional population consists of individuals whose illegal behavior involves contravention of laws governing the distribution and consumption of alcohol. Alcohol use precedes the criminal acts of a high percentage of offenders and many commit criminal acts only while under the influence of alcohol. The number of offenders who have alcohol-related behavioral or social problems, or who are addicted to alcohol, is substantial. A large number have drinking problems which seriously interfere with their ability to function socially in a *non*-criminal manner. Alcohol use is also associated with parole failure and recidivism. Accordingly, correctional agencies are under considerable obligation to provide programs in both institutional and community settings for the treatment of a large number of offenders whose criminal behavior is directly or indirectly related to alcohol abuse.

There is an extensive literature on the relationship between crime and alcohol. Surprisingly, this literature includes no adequate review of the nature, variety, quality or efficacy of alcohol-treatment programs in correctional settings. This book attempts to fill that gap. On the basis of an examination of the literature on alcohol treatment with offenders, we describe the nature and variety of programs which have been reported during the past decade, and critically review the efficacy of these programs.[1] Our review of the literature sought to identify programs which have been found to be effective in ameliorating the alcohol-related behavior problems of offenders or decreasing their post-treatment criminal behavior. It also attempted to identify program components and practices which are associated with a positive program outcome.

In order to provide a perspective, the book briefly reviews the evidence of an alcohol/crime link (Chapter 2) and summarizes research on the prevalence of drinking problems among offenders (Chapter 3).

WHILE WE ARE WAITING

We make no apology to those who would argue that the treatment of alcohol-abusing offenders is an inadequate response to the problems of alcohol-related crime. We have no argument with the view that the prevention of both alcohol abuse and crime requires not only changing offenders, but also changing the host of political, economic, social and cultural factors which play a major role in engendering these problems. We certainly would not quarrel with the conclusion that a clarification or a re-working of society's attitude towards drinking and drunkenness (particularly in relation to drinking and driving) is required before any significant effects on the rate of alcohol-related crime will be achieved.

> "Amid the jingling of cash registers in our Government-owned liquor stores, we hear the annual Government declaration of war on drinking and driving" (Orland French, 1984).

We consider it totally justifiable to concern ourselves with changing offenders who some would argue are "victims" of adverse social conditions while patiently waiting or hoping for change in such social conditions. We do not feel we need to rationalize attempts to change offenders whose alcohol-related behavior may continue to produce problems for others which are far more severe than any of the problems that they themselves have experienced.

TREATMENT VS. DETERRENCE

Our focus on the treatment of offenders with alcohol-related problems is not meant to deny the value of attempting to prevent alcohol-related crime through deterrence, i.e. by increasing the certainty of apprehension and the severity of punishment for alcohol-related crimes, particularly "driving-while-impaired."

Punishment is, of course, the oldest and most popular approach of the criminal justice system. It is based on the assumption that offenders, or potential offenders, are rational persons who would choose not to commit crimes if the risk of being caught and convicted was high and the punishment they would receive would outweigh the possible gains their crimes could yield. Deterrence advocates recommend increasing the powers or the resources of police to augment the probability of apprehension, increasing the probability that arrests lead to convictions, increasing the probability that convictions lead to punishment and increasing the severity of punishment (including increasing the frequency and length of prison sentences).

Regrettably, research on the efficacy of deterrence does not justify optimism for this approach to alcohol-related crimes (Blumstein, Cohen & Nagin, 1978; Fattah, 1982; Hagan, 1982; Gendreau & Ross, 1981; Gibbs, 1982; Ross & Gendreau, 1983). Very low correlations have been found between crime rate and the certainty of apprehension or the severity of punishment. Sometimes the correlations have been negative, i.e. the greater the chances of being caught and punished, the *higher* the crime rate! Deterrent effects are frequently unreliable and weak. Moreover, the strongest of these weak effects are for minor offences. Highly conflicting results have been found for deterrence programs aimed at decreasing the incidence of major offences. Deterrence effects, when they are achieved, are typically only temporary. Often they serve only to change the kind of crime committed to those which have not been made a focus of attention. Sometimes, they only serve to shift crime to another geographic location.

Increasing the length of prison sentences has very little effect on crime rates and increasing the use of prison sentences greatly increases already present problems of prisons: overcrowding and costs. The achievement of even a 1% reduction in crime might require an increase in costs of as much as 300% to 500%. The costs of increased deterrence in terms of police and court budgets is also staggering; the results far from guaranteed. Moreover, increases in rates of apprehension and rates of conviction are by no means easy to achieve, regardless of budgetary considerations. Increasing the certainty and severity of aversive consequences of alcohol-related crime is appealing but it is a deceptively simple solution to a complex problem.

From a psychological perspective, deterrence has little reality or meaning for many offenders. Many offenders seldom consider the consequences of their acts (Ross & Fabiano, 1981; 1985). Many underestimate the risks. Some are indifferent to the risks. Some thrive on them. Many are sublimely optimistic; they believe that they will not be caught; if caught, not convicted; if convicted, not sentenced; if sentenced, not imprisoned; if imprisoned, quickly released. Such beliefs are by no means unrealistic.

Moreover, there are large individual differences in people's response to punishment or threat of punishment. Many of the punishments which society is prepared to use may not be even mildly aversive to some offenders. It is not a simple matter to convince potential offenders that "we mean business." This is particularly the case when their realization of (or concern for) the possible consequences of their behavior as well as their judgement of the aversiveness of the penalties and the risks involved have been temporarily or permanently impaired by their ingestion of alcohol.

In short, research has indicated that deterrence is a poorly understood, highly complicated approach to crime prevention and one which can be difficult to operationalize, inordinately expensive, and questionably effective. However, our lack of enthusiasm for a simple deterrence model does not mean that we view criminal sanctions as unimportant. They may not be a *sufficient* response to alcohol-related crimes, only an *essential* one. Research has indicated that an essential component of effective treatment programs for offenders is training them to consider the consequences of their behavior before they act (Ross & Fabiano, 1985). Moreover, in the treatment of those offenders who abuse alcohol, confronting them with the consequences of their drinking may be a *crucial* step towards the modification of their behavior. Treatment of offenders does not mean molly-coddling. Treatment and deterrence are not incompatible.

ALCOHOL PROGRAMS FOR NON-OFFENDERS

Although we focus our discussion of the efficacy of alcohol-abuse treatment on programs for offender populations, limiting the discussion to such populations would be both unrealistic and misleading. Self-report studies (and a little common-sense) have made it abundantly clear that individuals who are officially and formally labelled as offenders are by no means the only offenders in our society. They are the ones who have been apprehended and convicted of acts which have been defined as illegal and which, for whatever reason, have concerned the police and the criminal justice system enough to take action. Many "non-offenders" who have alcohol-related problems may also have been engaged in a variety of criminal activities which have not led to their involvement with the criminal justice system. Accordingly, while focussing on programs for official offenders we do so in the context of a brief assessment of the efficacy of alcohol-abuse programs for the general population (Chapter 6).

Our discussion of research on alcohol-abuse programs for the general population is particularly salient when one considers that society has varied considerably over the years in its view as to whether various forms of behavior exhibited under the influence of alcohol is or is not criminal. There has also been considerable variation in society's determination as to which agency should respond to such behavior (criminal justice system, health services, psychiatric services, social service agencies . . .). Accordingly, much of the treatment for official offenders with alcohol-related problems has been provided by treatment agencies outside of the correctional or criminal justice system. Reports on such programs seldom differentiate the outcome for offenders from those of their non-offender clients. However, to dismiss them on those grounds would be to ignore a substantial number of programs which provide service for alcohol-abusing offenders.

OFFENDER REHABILITATION

Many, perhaps most, of the offenders who evidence problem drinking have a number of other cognitive/emotional/behavioral and environmental/social problems which may be a cause of their alcohol abuse. In addition, many of them may also be dependent on other drugs as well as alcohol and may well require treatment not only for alcohol-abuse but for multiple substance-abuse. It is less than wise to attempt to limit the treatment of these individuals to their drinking behavior without dealing with their other problems. Treatment of the alcohol-abusing offender must be comprehensive; we simply cannot treat one aspect of the offender while ignoring the others. Similarly, an adequate understanding of the efficacy of the alcohol-abuse treatment for offenders must include consideration of the efficacy of correctional treatment in general. This, of course, is a topic of considerable controversy, as we shall see in Chapter 4 in which we discuss the "nothing works" debate: the long-standing argument about whether or not treatment of offenders has had any significant impact on their criminal behavior.

ALCOHOL, ABUSE & TREATMENT: PRINCIPLES & RECOMMENDATIONS

To set the stage for our discussion of the efficacy of alcohol-abuse treatment we present, in Chapter 5, a brief description of the nature of alcohol and its effects. We also discuss the meaning of the wide variety of terms which have been used to categorize individuals whose use of alcohol is associated with social and behavioral problems. We return to the discussion of these topics in Chapter 8 in which we present some guidelines for the development of alcohol-abuse programs for correctional populations. In presenting these recommendations we note that the efficacy of programs depends not only on the intensity of the program, its nature and the quality, competence, motivation, and industriousness of its staff, but also on the adequacy of the program's conceptualization of the effects of alcohol and the causes of alcohol abuse. It also depends on the degree to which the specific programs which are delivered to particular groups of clients are those for whom such programs are appropriate.

The focus of our research has been on identifying programs which have been demonstrated in methodologically adequate research to be effective in reducing the alcohol abuse and/or the criminal behavior of offenders. Programs which have not been adequately evaluated are given short shrift. This does not mean that they do not "work" but only that we cannot determine if they do. Many of the programs currently being provided may be highly efficacious; some may be harmful. Without an adequate evaluation it is too easy to mistake one for the other. Accordingly, in the final chapter we present suggestions for evaluating correctional alcohol abuse programs.

CHAPTER 2

THE ALCOHOL/CRIME CONNECTION

ALCOHOL & VIOLENCE

THERE is ample evidence that alcohol use by the offender or the victim, or both, precedes a high proportion of violent criminal acts (Pernanen, 1976; Roizen & Schneberk, 1977). Alcohol is implicated in as many as 53% to 64% of cases of homicide (Voss & Hepburn, 1968; Wolfgang, 1958), and in 34% to 72% of cases of rape (Amir, 1971; Johnson, Gibson & Linden, 1978; Rada, 1975). As many as 58% of offenders convicted of assault were drinking at the time of the offence (Mayfield, 1976). Sixty-four per cent of offenders convicted of assaulting police were drinking or drunk at the time of the offence (Meyer, Magendanz, Kieselhorst, & Chapman, 1978).

A survey of state prisons in the U.S. found that 34% to 45% of offenders convicted of a violent offence (homicide, assault, rape, robbery) described themselves as very heavy drinkers (Kalish, 1983). A study of violence in Sweden found that 68% of the offenders were intoxicated when committing their violent act (Roslund & Larson, 1979). In Canada, Pernanen (1979) found that in 52% of violent incidents at least one of the participatns was drinking. MacDonald & Bygott's (1977) study of murders in Canada concluded that 35% involved alcohol.

A relationship between alcohol use and violence is also strongly suggested by the fact that rates of violent crime decrease with decreased availability of alcohol (Lenke, 1975; Takala, 1973). Moreover, higher levels of alcohol consumption are more likely to be linked to violent crime than are lower levels (Shupe, 1954; Tinklenberg, 1973)[2].

Although societal views of violent crime often fail to include personal injury or death resulting from driving while impaired, drunk drivers are responsible for approximately half of all traffic fatalities (Jones, 1977). As Morris and Hawkins (1970) point out, drunk driving is a more common cause of death than is "intentional" violence.

VIOLENCE IN: VIOLENCE OUT

A relationship between alcohol abuse and family violence has been well documented (Hamilton & Collins, 1981). The precise nature of the relationship is not well understood, but there is little doubt that alcohol plays an important role in family violence, particularly in cases of spouse abuse.[3] Spouse and/or child abusing males are more likely than the general population to be alcohol abusers and the highest rates of family violence are found among moderate to heavy drinkers. In fact, drunkenness in one party appears to be the best predictor of family violence (Byles, 1978).

The link between alcohol abuse and family violence is particularly significant in view of the fact that the *experience* of violence in childhood is a frequent precursor of the *expression* of violence in adulthood (Ross, 1980). Many child-abusing adults were themselves victims of parental violence in their childhood and/or witnessed violence between their parents (Bakan, 1971; Gelles, 1973; Gil, 1971; Silver, Dublin & Louri, 1969). The early life of many murderers is characterized by child abuse and violence between parents (Duncan & Duncan, 1971; Palmer, 1962; Tanay, 1969). Similarly, the adult who is violent towards his spouse is likely to have been a witness of assaultive behavior between his own parents or a target of their violence (Ball, 1977; Flynn, 1977; Gelles, 1974). In effect, the more individuals are exposed to violence as children (as observers or as victims), the more likely are they as adults to be violent towards other people, including their spouses and/or their children. Since many of the violent incidents to which children are exposed in early life are associated with alcohol abuse, and since the victims of such violence may later become violent to others, it appears that alcohol abuse may have both a short-term and long-term relationship to violence. Moreover, recent evidence has demonstrated that exposure to violence in early life is associated with self-injurious behavior in later life. Children who have been victims of abuse may later become abusive not only to others but to themselves (Ross, 1980). It may well be that exposure to violence at the hands of alcohol-abusing parents may lead the victim to engage, in adulthood, in self-injurious behavior such as alcohol-abuse which, in turn, may engender violence towards others. Alcohol-related violence may beget alcohol-related violence.

OFFENSIVE DRINKING: ALCOHOL & NON-VIOLENT CRIME

Alcohol has also been found to be strongly associated with property offences. A survey of more than 10,000 inmates in correctional institutions in the U.S. found that a high percentage of offenders reported that they were drinking at the time of the offence: robbery, 39%; larceny, 38%; auto theft, 46%; forgery, 38%; burglary, 47%; and arson, 67% (Roizen & Schneberk, 1977). Studies of incarcerated property offenders have reported that as many as 55% of those who reported drinking at the time of their offence were "heavy drinkers" (Institute for Scientific Analysis, 1978).

A relationship between alcohol use and criminal behavior is also suggested by a variety of other research findings. It has been demonstrated, for example, that the greater the number of convictions for drunkenness, the more likely it is that the offender has had a non-alcohol-related criminal record (Lindelius & Salum, 1973). Moreover, both drinking and crime decrease with increasing age (Greenberg, 1981).

CAUSE, CORRELATE OR ARTIFACT?

Although there is abundant evidence to indicate that alcohol and criminal behavior are linked, the exact nature of the relationship remains ambiguous (Collins, 1981). It is by no means clear whether the often demonstrated relationship is casual or only statistical; whether alcohol use is a cause of crime or merely a correlate.

Methodological weaknesses in the research on the alcohol/crime link seriously limit our understanding of whether and how alcohol use influences criminal behavior. The research shortcomings include poor or non-standardized definitions of both alcohol use and crime. Extreme and biased samples of offenders (particularly prison samples) have frequently been used. Researchers have too often depended on self-reports of alcohol use and they typically have failed to use reliable measures of drinking. Estimates of the strength of the relationship are also influenced by police discretion; differential handling by the police (and the courts) can result in alcohol abusing individuals being over or under-represented in official statistics.

There is very little evidence which would substantiate the assumption that alcohol is a *cause* of crime except in those occasional cases of "pathological intoxication" in which explosive out-bursts of violence occur with the ingestion of even small amounts of alcohol (Bach-y-Rita, Lion & Ervin, 1970; Cuthbert, 1970; Macinacci, 1963; Skelton, 1970). Even in such cases, other factors (personality, neurological and situational variables) appear to be involved (Collins, 1981). It is more likely that alcohol use is a *contributing* rather than a causative factor in criminal behavior. The available evidence suggests that it is a determinant rather than a cause of crime. Most people who drink do not commit crimes.

Alcohol use may predispose some individuals to criminal behavior through its impact on other factors which in some instances may be associated with violent behavior, e.g. hypoglycemia (Herman, Sesko, Trinajstic, Vidovic, & Cabrijan, 1970; Moynihan, 1965; Vartia, Forsander, & Drusius, 1960); temporal lobe dysfunction (Pernanen, 1981); or REM sleep deprivation (Gove, 1969; Johnson, Burdick, & Smith, 1970). Long-term alcohol abuse may engender physiological changes which decrease the individual's ability to cope without engaging in criminal behavior (Pernanen, 1981). Furthermore, social definitions of drinking events as occasions for licence may lead the individual into criminal activity (MacAndrew & Edgerton, 1969). The effect of alcohol ingestion on perceptual/cognitive functions may lead the individual to misread social situations, particularly conflict situations, and may impair his judgement and increase his risk-taking (Epstein & Taylor, 1967; Pernanen, 1976). In turn, public attitudes towards the individual who has been drinking may increase the probability of confrontation of a violent nature. It may also increase the frequency of various antagonistic behaviors which can lead to interpersonal friction (argumentative, loud, inconsiderate behavior) (Pernanen, 1976). There may also be a situational explanation for the alcohol-crime link. Drinking often occurs in bars and pubs and other places where offenders congregate. The link may reflect not physiological or psychological effects of alcohol but merely that its use is correlated with occasions when the individual associates with other offenders in situations where criminal acts are discussed.

> "Circumstances of drinking produce greater changes in behavior than the alcohol does" (Carpenter & Armenti, 1972, p. 540).

Finally, drinking may act simply to provide the offender with an excuse to behave in an antisocial manner. For example, Coleman & Strauss (1979) found that abusive husbands sometimes drink alcohol so that they then can blame drunkenness for their inclination to beat their wives.

Another possibility is that the association between alcohol abuse and criminal behavior does not indicate that alcohol is a *cause* of crime but simply demonstrates that alcohol abuse and criminal behavior are related to the same underlying factors (e.g. socio-economic background, inadequate socialization, impulsivity, risk-taking, low frustration tolerance, parental neglect, or inadequate parental role models).

On the other hand, the link between alcohol use and crime may be artifactual. The relationship may actually be a link between being a drinker and being caught rather than between being a drinker and being a criminal. Offenders who have been drinking have a higher risk of being caught than nondrinking offenders (Petersilia, Greenwood, & Lavin, 1978). This may be because when they are drinking their behavior is more noticeable. It may be that their lowered motor coordination and reaction time impedes their avoiding apprehension, or that their impaired judgement causes them to leave clues or to take risks which increase the likelihood of detection. Finally, it may be that their drinking history may make them well known to the police (Pernanen, 1981).[4]

Studies which report a high prevalence of drinking problems among offender populations have almost exclusively utilized prison samples. Since considerably less than 5% of all the crimes committed lead to the incarceration of an offender, and since young, serious or persistent offenders are overrepresented in prison populations, these studies give a highly biased impression of the crime/alcohol link. Their results may more properly reflect a relationship between alcohol use and sentencing and incarcerating, or between alcohol use and *serious* crime. Complicating the matter further has been the tendency of investigators to fail to compare their prison samples with non-offenders with similar social-demographic characteristics.

ALCOHOLISM/CRIME LOTTERY

Doubts about the relationship are also raised by the inconsistencies among studies of criminal activities in alcoholic populations. Such studies report that among populations of alcoholics the proportions of individuals with criminal records range from 10% to 90%! (Greenberg, 1981). Although alcoholics may have a higher level of criminality than the general population, alcoholism is never a necessary and is seldom a sufficient cause of criminal behavior.

The reliance or self-report techniques in studies of offenders may lead to an over-estimation of the strength of the alcohol/crime link. Offenders may erroneously report the use of alcohol in an attempt to deny their responsibility for a criminal act. Moreover, at least one study found that many of the offenders who were drunk at the time of their offence thought that their use of alcohol was irrelevant to their criminal behavior (Mayfield, 1976).

It should be noted that alcohol use may have a *suppressing* effect on criminal behavior. It may depress the motivation for some crimes. It may reduce the ability to perform some crimes e.g. computer-crimes, embezzlement and other white-collar crimes. It may lead the individual to more passive forms of behavior, and may actually *prevent* some crime by incapacitating the potential offender (Merton, 1957; Roizen & Schneberk, 1977a). Studies which have shown that offenders who were drinking at the time of their offence almost always fail to seek information on how often when they were drinking they did *not* commit criminal acts. The vast majority of drinking occasions are not followed by antisocial or criminal behavior. Alcohol has often been blamed for crime without sufficient justification.

The relationship between alcohol and criminal behavior is complex and poorly understood. However, while bearing in mind the foregoing caveats, it seems reasonable to conclude that there is a strong association between alcohol crime both for minor offences and serious offences. Moreover, as we shall discuss in the next chapter, there is little doubt that there are a substantial number of offenders whose problems include or are related to their abuse of alcohol.

CHAPTER 3

PREVALENCE OF ALCOHOL ABUSE AMONG OFFENDERS

PRECISE estimates of the number of offenders whose problems are related to their use or abuse of alcohol are not possible. This is primarily because of definition and classification problems. A multitude of ill-defined terms such as "alcohol addict," "problem drinker," "alcohol-abuser," "alcoholic," "intemperate" have been used, often indiscriminately and sometimes pejoratively, to describe offenders who have been drinking. Each of these terms has been used to categorize a wide variety of individuals who vary greatly in amount, pattern or style of drinking and in the physiological or social consequences of their drinking. Seldom do the reports explain what the terms they use mean. When they do, there is seldom agreement from one study to the next as to the meaning of common terms. Complicating the matter further is the fact that different studies not only include a wide range of types of drinkers, but also a wide range of offenders. The offenders studied range from those involved in major offences to those whose only "offence" was being drunk. Some have no criminal history beyond liquor violations; others have lengthy criminal records. Many studies simply fail to indicate the characteristics of their subjects either in terms of criminal behavior or drinking behavior. Most fail to indicate the criteria used for the labels they apply and one is left to guess what is meant by these terms. It is simply not possible in most cases to compare the findings of one study with another. Attempting to make sense out of this literature is a formidable task.

Estimates of alcoholism[5] in the correctional population depend on the type of crime committed. In various studies, estimates range between 21% – 30% in cases of homicide, robbery, and burglary; between 0% and 40% in sex offences; and between 11% and 30% in cases of larceny (cf. Greenberg, 1981). For unspecified crimes, the estimates range from 40% to 60%. However, most studies of the prevalence of alcoholism, no matter how defined, have used prison samples. These may yield over-estimates of alcoholism. Nonetheless they do indicate that one group of offenders (those in institutions) have a high rate of alcoholism. This rate has been shown to be higher than the rate of alcoholism in the general population (Roizen & Schneberk, 1977). If prison samples are compared to samples of the general population with similar demographic characteristics these differences might not be as great, but they would still indicate that the prevalence of alcoholism in the prison population is significant.

Actually, the prevalence of "alcoholics" or *chronic* alcohol abusers in the offender population may be less important than the number of offenders who exhibit *acute* excessive drinking. The latter may be more relevant to a criminal lifestyle than is "alcoholism" (Cook, 1962; Goodwin, 1973). There are also many offenders who do not drink excessively or frequently, but when they do drink, do so incautiously. Some, not realizing the interaction of alcohol and physiological conditions, drink injudiciously. Many offenders are viewed as problem drinkers on the basis of what *might* be an isolated event (e.g. a drinking offence). Some offenders have a long history of both criminal behavior and alcohol abuse. Other offenders have no criminal history except for alcohol-related traffic offences or breaches of liquor laws. There is no one term to subsume all these different types of individuals who may need differing amounts and types of treatment . . . or none at all. In the present report we will use the general term "alcohol-abusing offender" except when reviewing reports which clearly specify that the clients were alcoholics, problem-drinkers, etc.

"FIRST HE KILLED THE BOTTLE"

Impaired drivers account for some 50% of fatal motor vehicle accidents which in North America result in more than 25,000 deaths annually (Erskine, 1972).

"ON THE ROCKS"

The prevalence of problem-drinking among offenders varies with the nature and location of the particular correctional setting studied.

Offenders with drinking problems are more likely to receive prison sentences and longer sentences than are other offenders convicted of the same crime (Vera Institute of Justice, 1977). Well's (1973) study of the inmate population in California reviewed that 75% had a history of drinking problems. Erskine (1972) found that no less than one half of the U.S. penitentiary population have long histories of excessive alcohol use. The pioneering study by Bannay, 1972) on three thousand admissions to Sing Sing Penitentiary over a two-year period led him to conclude that 22% had drinking problems. Some specific surveys of inmates incarcerated for serious felonies have found that problem drinking is seven to eight times higher than among the general population (Guze, Tuason, Gatfield, Stewart & Picken, 1962; Roth, Rosenberg, & Levinson, 1971).

It is not just among serious offenders that drinking problems are common. Despite the trend to decriminalization of public inebriation and the use of detoxification centers, arrests for public intoxication represent one of the highest crime categories in many jurisdictions (Erskine, 1972; NIAA, 1977). Between one third and one half of the inmates of American correctional institutions are there for the violation of laws regulating public intoxication (Winick, 1979). Many of these offenders have been arrested and jailed for short periods so often that they have served ten to twenty years without any treatment (President's Commission, 1970).

A 1979 Bureau of Justice Statistics Inmate Survey consisting of personal interviews with a stratified random sample of 12,000 inmates in U.S. state prisons is the first and only national assessment of offender alcohol use habits conducted to date. The results of this survey suggested that alcohol/drug abuse was a problem of "staggering size" (Department of Justice, 1983).

Inmate drinking habits were assessed with the following three measures:

1) frequency of drinking in the year prior to incarceration,
2) usual drinking amount: heavy drinkers were defined as those drinking 4 oz. absolute alcohol[6];
3) self-assessed degree of intoxication when finished drinking (using a four point scale from "relatively sober" to "very drunk").

Inmate drinking habits were compared to the norms for the general population with the following findings: Fifty percent of inmates drink an average of 1 oz. ethanol daily, compared to 10% of persons above 18 years of age in the general population. A smaller proportion of inmates (17%) were abstinent than was observed in the general population (33%). Men in prison were approximately 3 times as likely as men in general to drink an ounce or more of ethanol daily. Although female inmates drank much less than did males, they drank more heavily (5 times) than women in the general population.

The authors note that many inmates were heavily involved in drinking (i.e. daily and/or heavy drinking) in the year before they entered prison. Approximately one-third of inmates were daily drinkers, and two-thirds of these were heavy drinkers. Thirty percent of the offenders reported that they had engaged in heavy drinking just prior to the commission of their offence; but such heavy consumption was not an unusual event — for many offenders, consuming 9 ounces of 40% alcohol was their typical drinking pattern! Heavy drinkers were more likely to be habitual offenders (convicted of more than 5 offences) and to have been convicted of the crimes of assault, burglary and rape.

It should be noted that most of the data in the national survey consisted of inmate self-reports. One would be wise to have some reservations about the reliability of such data. However, a recent study of inmates in the New York State Department of Corrections indicates that self-report data may *under*estimate the actual alcohol abuse problem among offenders. Whereas self-report data indicated that only 19% had alcohol abuse problems, an alcohol screening test

(MAST) revealed that 35% had such problems (Grossman & MacDonald, 1983).

In the national study it was found that among inmates who reported drinking in the year prior to incarceration, only about 20% had ever been involved in an alcohol treatment program. *Seventy percent of habitual heavy drinkers reported no previous addictions treatment experience.*

ALCOHOL & REHABILITATION

Alcohol use has been found to be an effective predictor of parole failure (NCCD, 1972) and of poor adjustment in half-way houses (Moczydlowski, 1980). Alcohol use has also been found to be a significant determining factor in recidivism (Guze & Cantwell, 1965; Goodwin, Crane & Guze, 1971; Evard, 1971; Lambert& Madden, 1975; Waller, 1974). Moreover, favourable parole decisions for an alcohol abusing inmate are often contingent upon whether or not he is undergoing therapy (Glaser & O'Leary, 1973; Madden, 1980).

In a prolonged criminal career, the influence of alcohol is overwhelming. Guze *et al.*, (1962, 1969) found in his examination of 233 career inmates that no less than 43% had a severe drinking problem. Alcohol was the single most important problem associated with their persistent criminal behavior.

The necessity for the implementation of treatment programs is apparent. The question remains, how effective can such programs be?

CHAPTER 4

THE REHABILITATION OF CORRECTIONAL TREATMENT

THE most frequently quoted and most seldom read text in the criminological literature is probably an article published in 1974 in the *Public Interest* by the sociologist, Robert Martinson. Martinson's article was a research report which, unlike most research reports in the field of criminal justice, had a widespread and profound impact on criminal justice policy and correctional practice. In brief, Martinson reported that an extensive review of 231 studies of research on correctional rehabilitation programs had yielded convincing evidence that most programs fail to reduce crime and fail to reduce the recidivism of juvenile or adult offenders. In correctional rehabilitation, Martinson declared, "almost nothing works"; "correctional treatment is impotent."

Martinson was the most outspoken, the most vociferous, the most dramatic and the most persuasive critic of correctional treatment, but he was neither the first nor the only critic of a rehabilitation approach to criminal behavior. Much earlier, Bailey's (1966) examination of correctional programs had led him to conclude that "evidence supporting the efficacy of correctional programs is slight, inconsistent, and of questionable reliability." Robinson & Smith (1971) asserted that "there is no evidence to support any program's claim to superior rehabilitative efficacy." Kassebaum, Ward & Wilner (1971) announced on the basis of their review that "as the reports come in, there is a dearth of good tidings for both the program specialists and the program administrators." More recent reviews have echoed Martinson's well publicized conclusions. For example, Romig (1978) asserted:

> "Behavior modificaton should not be offered as a treatment modality . . . casework should be discontinued . . . group counselling should not be relied upon as a vehicle to rehabilitate . . . individual counselling and psychotherapy should be discontinued . . . rehabilitation programs that focus on the teaching of academic skills will fail to reduce recidivism . . . "

Romig added to his list of "failures": job placement, vocational training, occupational orientation, and work programs. Many other reviewers of correctional treatment research joined in the "nothing works" chorus (e.g. Fishman, 1977; Greenberg, 1977).

It's An Ill Wind . . .

It is unlikely that Martinson and his fellow critics could foresee the impact that their condemnation of correctional treatment was to engender. They merely had put treatment on trial and found it guilty of fraud and misrepresentation, or at least of existing without visible means of support. They did not pronounce the sentence. It remained for others to advise what should be done to make corrections mend its ways.

The conclusion that treatment of the offender is an ineffective response to criminal behavior was eagerly endorsed by many, perhaps most academics and criminal justice policy makers and administrators. Many interpreted the apparent failure of correctional rehabilitation programs as *prima facie* evidence for the view that treatment is an inappropriate response to crime: we were treating the wrong problem. Rather than treating offenders, it was asserted, we should be treating social conditions such as poverty, class conflict, unemployment and the like which are the "real" causes of crime. The failure of correctional treatment was to be expected because, they asserted, it was based on an erroneous model of crime: the medical model which ascribed criminal behavior to some presumed illness in the offender rather than to social/political/economic ills.

Many were gratified by the apparent failure of a helping approach to offenders which they interpreted as molly-coddling individuals who needed to be handled firmly, if not punitively. In contrast, other more sanguine individuals welcomed the news of the failure of an approach which they saw as engendering blatantly unjust practices. They were heartened to learn that no longer could the benefits of decreased recidivism be used to justify such deprivations of human rights and human dignity as was engendered by involuntary participation in treatment (particularly the behavior modification brand of treatment). They noted that treatment only *sounded* benign. Sometimes treatment provided a euphemism for repugnant practices which were more manipulative, dehumanizing, and punitive than were entailed under more retributive regimes (Ross & McKay, 1979).

Treating or Aging?

> "And to hell with another headshrinker. All they do is get a guy more time" (Elli, 1966).

The apparent failure of correctional rehabilitation raised further doubts about the value and rationale of indeterminate sentencing by which offenders were incarcerated for indefinite periods of time, i.e., until they were judged to have been "cured." How, the critics asked, could we continue this practice when it was based on two faulty premises: (1) the assumption that correctional agents could make valid judgement about when and whether an offender was rehabilitated and ready for release, and (2) the assumption that *mandatory* treatment could be effective in rehabilitating offenders (particularly in prisons). The failure of treatment destroyed the last vestige of rationality from a practice which, its detractors claimed, made justice too capricious. "I sentence you," says the judge, "but to what I know not . . ." (Coleman, 1948). Treatment, it was argued, served merely to increase the length of time the offender spent in prison. It did so arbitrarily and without gain either to the offender or society. Support grew for fixed sentences (e.g. Boland & Wilson, 1978; Fogel, 1975).

> "They are not punishing, not inflicting, only healing. But do not let us be deceived by a name . . . to undergo all those assaults on my personality which modern psychotherapy knows how to deliver; to be re-made after some pattern of 'normality' hatched

in a Viennese Laboratory to which I never professed allegiance; to know that this process will never end until either my captors have succeeded or I have grown wise enough to cheat them with apparent success — who cares whether this is called treatment or not?" (Lewis, 1970).

In response to the "nothing works" verdict, some individuals suggested that we should stop intervening in the lives or minds of offenders; that we would be better off leaving them alone and pursuing a policy of "non-intervention" (Schur, 1973). Some proposed that corrections get out of the rehabilitation business and into the business of "carrying out the sentence of the court" rather than the recommendations of the psychiatrists. Some suggested we cease to coerce offenders into ineffective programs but, instead, provide these (same) programs only as "opportunities" which the offender was "free" to accept or reject based entirely on his own free will and volition (or his perception of the ensuing response of the parole board?). Charged with the failure of their programs, they did what any smart businessman would do: they limited their liability. Now the offender would be responsible for his failure and not correctional management which merely "offered" the (ineffective) programs.

Get Tough Models

"The remedy is to reject the ethic of a fake psychiatric therapeutism masquerading as the rehabilitation of offenders, and to reembrace the ethic of a truly dignified system of criminal sanctions consisting of minimal but fitting punishments meted out as inexorably and as fairly as possible" (Szasz, 1977).

Some advocated the abandonment of the treatment-rehabilitation model and urged that we progress to models which emphasize swift and certain penalties, deterrence, or retribution. It seemed to matter not a whit that the evidence for the effectiveness of these models (or *any* other correctional model) was even less than it was in the case of that which they were to supplant. The new models could be rationalized on other bases, including "justice and fairness":

"To be 'cured' against one's will and cured of states which we may not regard as disease is to be put on the level of those who have not yet reached the age of reason or those who never will; to be classed with infants, imbeciles, and domestic animals. But to be punished . . . because we have deserved it, because 'we ought to know better', is to be treated as a human person . . ." (Lewis, 1971).

The King is Dead: Long Live the King(s)

It could probably be argued that the apparent demise of treatment allowed other correctional practices such as restitution, fine options, community service orders, victim reconciliation, and the like to emerge or at least to prosper. Rehabilitation had failed. The research said it had. So we embarked on these "new" programs which were not "rehabilitation" programs . . . or were they? Although we declared that we were now in the business of ensuring that "justice" was being done to the offender, to his victim, and to his community, we still seemed to be in the business of correcting (changing) people. In some jurisdictions the rhetoric of rehabilitation became passé, but the practice continued. In some instances we remained in the rehabilitation business and simply changed our location: from the prison to the community[7]. Probation officers and others continued to urge their clients to participate in counselling, employment training, life-skills programs and the like. However, many correctional workers stopped being counsellors or therapists and became "brokers" who referred their clients for service to other agencies who, presumably, did what the probation officer used to do when corrections was in the treatment business and was responsible for changing offenders. Now the "broker" referred his clients to a cadre of lay people (volunteers) who were eager to help and who spent most of their time befriending, relating with, counselling and otherwise "treating" their clients in the same old, apparently, ineffective ways the paid staff had done before. The "nothing works" edict enabled corrections to attain in enviable position: having declared bankruptcy, it blithely announced it would continue in business but the responsibility for its success (or failure) would now have to be assumed by others.

The Bottom Line

Correctional administrators, hard pressed to maintain expensive treatment programs in a time of increasing financial constraints, were relieved to learn that such programs were ineffective. Austerity and the declared impotence of treatment combined to stimulate correctional managers to become concerned with shrinking budgets and allowed them to give short shrift to shrinking heads.

Additional Charges

It would be unfair to suggest that the dilemma of corrections was entirely attributable to Robert Martinson or to the other accademics who declared that corrections was not accomplishing its goals. The negative reviews were published at a time when corrections was being influenced very strongly by the fact that society in general was moving towards more conservative sentiments, was becoming disenchanted with the unrequited optimism of the 1960's, and was becoming preoccupied with fiscal acountability. Martinson may not have been the *deus ex machina* of the anti-treatment movement in corrections, but only its catalyst. His sweeping condemnation of corrections came at a time when the criminal justice system was in trouble. Crime rates had escalated dramatically . . . so had prison riots. The attack on treatment came at a time when corrections badly needed an overhaul. It also needed a scapegoat. Treatment became associated with coercion, long sentences, and prisons even though the majority of institutions proclaimed rehabilitation as their goal but provided barely a modicum of programs as their means to achieve such a goal. Somehow it came to be thought that it was not the deplorable conditions which were to blame for the troubles in prisons; it was the inappropriate model we had adopted: rehabilitation.

A Fair Trial?

Whereas many were gratified by the conclusions of the reviews of correctional outcome, others were somewhat less than enchanted. The assertions of the anti-rehabilitationists did not go unchallenged. In fact the "almost nothing works" pronouncements stimulated a heated and prolonged debate about the effectiveness of correctional treatment which has pre-occupied criminologists for more than a decade. Many questioned the validity of the negative conclusions about the outcome of correctional treatment (e.g. Adams, 1976; Chaneles, 1975; Gottfredson, 1980; Halleck & Witte, 1977; Klockars, 1975; Ross & McKay, 1978; Smith & Berlin, 1977).

It was argued that the reviewers had judged the successes and the failures of a program regardless of its nature, the setting in which it was conducted, its intensity, its duration, the type of offender to whom it was applied, or the characteristics of its staff: their training, their skills, their industriousness or their motivation. Programs conducted by poor staff were weighted equally with programs conducted by dedicated, well trained staff. Programs which purported to provide service but did so in name only, cancelled out programs in which quality service was *actually* provided. Many argued that the quality of evaluation research was inadequate to enable an unqualified conclusion that treatment was ineffective. It was pointed out that the "failed" programs were often of such poor quality that it was foolish to have thought that they had any hope of succeeding. It was noted that many programs were so poorly conceived that they were totally inappropriate and were bound to fail. Moreover, the reviews looked only at overall results. Programs which were successful with some offenders were declared ineffective if they did not work with other offenders for whom they may not have been appropriate. In fact, it was noted that the review actually identified a considerable number of successful programs. The lament of Martinson's detractors was that he had lumped together the outcome of good programs with that of extremely poor quality programs. Everything, good or bad, was thrown into an evaluation stew-pot. The stew tasted foul even though it contained some splendid ingredients. Perhaps it would have been more fitting to have recommended that we take more care in cooking, rather than that we should give up eating altogether.

Martinson's original pronouncements seemed to divide the correctional audience into opposing camps with firmly established positions: pro- or anti-treatment. All of the rebuttals probably did little more than entrench these positions even more strongly. It is not merely cynical to suggest that the position one took depended in large measure on one's profession, position and territory.

The positions were not noticeably changed even when Martinson repented. In 1979 he withdrew his conclusion that "almost nothing works." He rejected the methodology he had used to reach that conclusion, calling it "premature." He appealed his own verdict that treatment is "impotent":

> ". . . contrary to my previous position, some treatment programs do have an appreciable effect on recidivism . . . The evidence in our survey is simply too overwhelming to ignore" (Martinson, 1979).[8]

Martinson's earlier negative statements received far more attention than his revised positive statements about correctional treatment; a state of affairs not uncommon in corrections where good news is no news.

Ancient History

It is ironic that the conclusion that correctional treatment is ineffective is based on reviews of studies which were conducted before 1967. Even the most recent reviews refer almost exclusively to the same pre-1967 literature (e.g. Romig, 1978). It should probably not surprise anyone that since 1967 there have been improvements both in the quality of the programs and in the quality of the procedures by which these programs have been evaluated.

New Evidence; New Trial

A review of the literature on programs conducted between 1973 and 1978 revealed that there are a considerable number of programs which have been demonstrated in methodologically impressive research to be effective in offender rehabilitation (Gendreau & Ross, 1979; Ross & Gendreau, 1980). The results of these programs are by no means trivial. In some studies, reductions in recidivism ranged from 30% – 60% (e.g., Alexander & Parsons, 1973; Chandler, 1980; Lee & Haynes, 1980; Phillips, Phillips, Fixsen & Wolff, 1973; Ross & McKay, 1976; Walter & Mills, 1979). The beneficial effects are not short-lived. Positive results have been found for as long as 3 to 15 years after treatment (Blakely, Davidson & Saylor, 1980; Jeffrey & Woolpert, 1974; O'Donnell, Lydgate & Fo, 1979; Sarason & Ganzer, 1980; Shore & Massimo, 1979). Successful programs involve not just "soft" delinquents but also hard-core offenders. The evaluation of these programs employed both randomized experimental and quasi-experimental designs which are at least as good and often better than the vast majority of studies evaluating the criminal justice system's efforts in any other endeavour including deterrence (Gendreau & Ross, 1981).

The general conclusion of the 1973-78 review was that there is convincing evidence that some programs when they are applied with integrity by competent practitioners to appropriate groups of offenders, can be effective in reducing recidivism. Most of the programs were also effective when measured by other criteria such as seriousness of anti-social behavior, employment stability, and family relations.

All Is Not Found

It must be stressed that not all programs are effective. Effective programs are probably well outnumbered by correctional programs which have failed. Programs which are ill-conceived, poorly implemented by unqualified staff or applied to inappropriate targets have (no matter how expensive or impressively packaged) little hope of achieving much beyond short-term publicity and the wasteful expenditure of public funds. Such programs are by no means uncommon. They may be the norm in a criminal justice system which is always too eager to adopt new remedies.

Nor are the effective programs which were identified in the 1973-78 review representative of the general state of the art in correctional treatment. The vast majority of correctional programs never were and still are not conducted in a scientific framework; their results have never been stringently evaluated and they have been systematically excluded from all of the reviews of the treatment literature. The reviews deal exclusively with programs which meet rigid standards of evaluation quality (if not program quality). Accordingly, most correctional programs have been totally discounted. Those who conclude that correctional treatment does not work have found most correctional programs guilty without a hearing. The nothing works proponents committed the cardinal academic sin: they asserted that they had proved the null hypothesis.

It should not be thought that when the 1973-78 review found a considerable number of programs which worked that the findings represented an endorsement of correctional treatment in general. Unsuccessful programs are not rare. They may be the rule. Effective programs are exceptional both in their results and in quality of their program efforts.

PROGRAM PRINCIPLES

The 1973-78 review identified some programs which significantly reduced recidivism and it provided a worthwhile service by making criminologists and criminal justice policy makers aware of specific programs which have "worked." However, it is important to go beyond description of specific programs to the application of the principles of effective correctional programming, to determine the characteristics which differentiate effective from ineffective programs, and to ascertain the essential components of programs which "work." Research on these questions is far from final but there are some guidelines which can be suggested at this stage. In general, it appears that the likelihood that a program will be effective depends on who does what to whom, where, why, for how long, with what intensity, and for what purpose.

Therapy or Teaching?

Much of the criticism of the treatment approach to offender rehabilitation is based on rejection of the conceptual model on which treatment programs are thought to be based: the much maligned medical model. Interestingly, of the many effective programs which have been described in the post-1973 literature, not one is based on a medical model.[9] Effective programs are based on a much more sound conceptualization of criminal behavior. They view the offender's behavior not simply as a symptom of some disease but as a consequence of a variety of social, economic, situational, cognitive, and behavioral factors which are known to be functionally related to delinquent behavior. Their efforts are directed towards modifying those aspects of the offender's environment or his behavior (intermediate targets) which are known to be correlated with recidivism. They focus on modifying well-defined behaviors, changing anti-social attitudes, correcting faulty thinking or inappropriate social perception, and developing adaptive interpersonal or vocational skills.

It is, perhaps, unfortunate that the effective programs are referred to as "treatment" programs since that implies illness, and therapy and the medical model.[10] In fact, most of the programs are based on a social learning model and consist of techniques designed to teach new skills and attitudes rather than curing diseases. They involve training and education (broadly conceived) rather than therapy.

Successful programs do not attempt major personality change. They are not so ambitious. They set more realistic goals. They target concrete, identifiable factors which are known to be associated with anti-social behavior. They are less ambitious than those programs touted as cures for crime in the days when we naively believed we could turn prisons into hospitals and prison guards into psychiatrists.

How To Treat?

Not surprisingly, we found no panaceas and no magic elixir that could be thought of as the "treatment-of-choice." Rather, we found a wide range of approaches which could be effective: contingency contracting, behavioral counselling, transactional analysis, family intervention, employment skills training, modelling and role-playing, peer group programs, social skills training and cognitive development training. The list is not exhaustive.

All of the effective programs were multi-facetted. They did not rely on any favourite single or simple method but, instead, incorporated a number of techniques. Not unlike offenders, effective programs are complex. There are no patent remedies.

Although a wide variety of treatment modalities have been used in effective correctional programs, recent research has revealed that one program component is common to almost every treatment effort which has been successful: cognitive development training (Ross & Fabiano, 1981; Ross & Fabiano, 1985). A component analysis revealed that effective programs differed significantly from ineffective programs in terms of their inclusion of techniques which would foster the development of the offender's thinking and reasoning skills, their social comprehension, and their problem-solving skills.

Attending to how the offender *thinks* may be at least as important as focussing on how he *feels* or how he *behaves*. Our analysis indicates that it may be valuable, even essential, to teach offenders to think logically, objectively and rationally without overgeneralizing, distorting the facts, or externalizing the blame. It is also important to train the offender to stop, think and analyze consequences before taking action; to teach him how to formulate plans and to more adequately conceptualize the means whereby he might satisfy his needs. Many offenders need to be taught how to analyze interpersonal problems, how to understand other people's values, behavior and feelings; how to recognize how their own behavior affects other people and why they respond to them as they do; and how to develop alternative, prosocial ways of reacting to interpersonal conflicts. A variety of programs and techniques have been developed to achieve such goals (Ross & Fabiano, 1983, Vol. 2).

Who Should Treat?

The 1973-78 review identified a sufficient number and variety of programs to constitute a menu for the correctional manager who might wish to try to replicate or extend a successful program in a new jurisdiction with new clients. However, there is, as yet, insufficient knowledge to enable the publication of a "recipe" for success although some particular ingredients appear to be required.

As might be expected, the characteristics of the correctional agent appears crucial. Not everyone can be effective. Earlier research (e.g. Truax & Carkhuff, 1967) suggested that the critical qualities of a therapist were his ability to express warmth, empathy, and unconditional positive regard for his client. Given the characteristics of some correctional clients, exceptionally tolerant workers seemed to be required!

However, more recent research seems to suggest that whereas

workers must be able to relate well to clients, it is perhaps less important that they be models of empathy than that they be models of prosocial behavior. Essential to the effectiveness of correctional programs are correctional workers who demonstrate to their clients socially acceptable ways of achieving goals. They teach or model non-criminal alternatives to those behaviors and attitudes which have led the offender into difficulty with the law. They also reinforce the anti-criminal attitudes and behaviors of their clients and correct their anti-social behaviors (Andrews & Kiessling, 1980; Sarason & Ganzer, 1980).

Effective treatment does not imply mollycoddling offenders. The effective staff member does not compromise the agency's rules but makes them clear and enforces them fairly and firmly (Andrews & Kiessling, 1980).

Many of the most effective programs are admirably cost-efficient. They do not require large numbers of highly qualified and highly paid professional staff. On the contrary, their "staff" consists mainly of college undergraduate and graduate students and other non-professional volunteers directed by a very small number of professionals. It is important to note that, in each instance, these individuals are carefully selected, well-trained and adequately supervised.

Whom To Treat?

There is a principle which would appear to be common-sensical but which has often been ignored by those who require that in order to be judged effective, treatment must "work" with all offenders. There is now clear evidence that the search for an across-the-board solution is futile. The search for panaceas fails to do justice to the variety of types of offenders. Offenders are a heterogeneous group. There are far more differences *among* offenders than there are *between* offenders and non-offenders. Different types of offenders need different types and different amounts of treatment. Many need no treatment at all. Their encounters with criminal sanctions are sufficient to dissuade them from further illegal activity. Others may "need" treatment but are likely to be totally unresponsive to any program. However, the prevention of criminal activity of many others requires their involvement in some form of correctional program. The likelihood of success for such involvement will depend on how well the program fits the particular characteristics of the offender. Research has demonstrated that some offenders may be harmed by some programs, i.e. their criminal activity may be *increased* as a result of their participation (e.g. O'Donnell, Lydgate & Fo, 1980). Research has also demonstrated that different types of offenders will respond differentially to different types of treatment (e.g. Jesness, 1975; O'Donnell, Lydgate & Fo, 1980). It is now recognized that effective correctional intervention requires careful matching of offender and intervention approach.

Where To Treat?

Many of the old, staid (and unsuccessful) programs treated offenders in a vaccuum. The client was seen in the privacy of the therapist's office and engaged in some kind of therapy for an hour or so each week. Many therapists believed that their therapeutic influence was sufficiently potent to overcome the negative environmental and social influences which their clients faced the other 113 hours in the week. There is very little evidence that their faith was justified. The self-esteem of the therapists was much higher than that of the offenders they treated.

It is clear that it is folly to think that a treatment program can be successful regardless of the setting in which it is conducted. Although there are some notable exceptions (e.g. Jesness, 1975; Platt, Perry & Metzger, 1980; Ross & McKay, 1976), the vast majority of effective programs identified in the 1973-78 review were conducted in community rather than institutional settings.

> "Unfortunately, there is no substantive relationship between . . . a lonely window-dressing counsellor and rehabilitation. Not while the majority of prisons supply "treatment" as an adjunct to punishment and degradation" (Griswold, 1970).

Some environments (not only institutional ones) are antagonistic to almost any kind of correctional program. the political, physical and social structure of the setting are key determinants of the outcome of a correctional program (and its tenure!). A program which hopes to succeed must be maximally adapted to the realities of the setting such that it is not incompatible with its environment. In some settings this means that no program will work. In some instances an adroit program manager can modify the correctional environment such that it is consonant with the program. In most instances it is the program which must be adapted to fit the demands of the correctional environment. Many programs have failed because of the setting or the policies of management or the lack of support of the correctional staff. Effective program managers must deal competently with the social/political realities of the treatment setting.

Program Integrity

Many of the programs which were judged to be ineffective were judged to be so on the basis of their application in projects which failed to ensure that the program was provided with sufficient intensity or for sufficient lengths of time to have any hope of success. Many employed untrained or poorly motivated staff. Many failed to ensure that the staff actually provided the service they were supposed to provide. Many failed to ensure that their program pactices were in accord with their program principles. In practice there often was no similarity between what the staff did and what the program principles (or even the title of the program) required that they do.

Effective programs, in contrast, are intensive programs. They provide high quality intervention for adequate periods of time. Program staff are not necessarily well paid but they are well trained and well supervised. Managers of effective programs make continuing efforts to ensure that their programs are not diluted or bastardized; the program practices conform to program principles, and that the services that are supposed to be provided (either by the treatment staff or cooperating agencies) *are* provided. They continually monitor to ensure that people practice what they preach. In short, a requirement for a good program is good management. Need we add that good management alone is no guarantee of good programs?

CONCLUSION

The debate about correctional effectiveness asked the question:

In correctional rehabilitation, does anything work? That question is no longer appropriate. The question has been answered in the affirmative. *Some* programs work very well with *some* offenders, with *some* staff, and in *some* settings.

Researchers who oppose the "nothing works" view have argued strongly and convincingly that assessment of the efficacy of correctional treatment should avoid summative research in which verdicts are made about efficacy in an across-the-board fashion and have recommended, instead, that assessment focus on the effectiveness of specific forms of intervention with specific types of offenders. Ironically, no assessment seems to have been made of the efficacy of various forms of treatment for a major sub-group of the offender population — those with alcohol-abuse problems.

CHAPTER 5

ALCOHOL, THE DRUG

BEFORE considering the nature and efficacy of treatment programs for alcohol-abusing offenders it is necessary to have a general understanding of how alcohol, the drug, affects human behavior and physiology after both short-term (acute) and long-term (chronic) usage.

Alcohol, or more precisely, ethyl alcohol, has been used by man probably since the dawn of civilization (Heath, 1975). Frequently the manner in which alcohol is used has been largely controlled by cultural and social forces. Different cultural groups are known to use alcohol in vastly differing frequencies and amounts. For example, high rates of "alcoholism" have been identified among Americans of Irish ancestry, while very low rates appear to characterize those of the Jewish faith (Bales, 1946; Knupfer & Room, 1967).

The significance of cultural factor is made clear by the fact that despite the almost universal use of alcohol by man, chronic abusive usage appears to be identified as a problem primarily in western industrialized society. Alcoholism, addiction and other pathological manifestations are extremely rare in cross-cultural perspective (Heath, 1975).

Definitions of alcoholism, alcohol abuse and addiction, as varied as they may be, typically refer to the social consequences of alcohol use as the major defining factors. Thus, alcohol exerts its effects upon an individual within the context not only of a particular individual with a unique set of genes and experiences, but also within the wider context of that individual's social, ethnic and cultural environment and heritage.

PREPARATION AND CONCENTRATION

No doubt contributing to alcohol's widespread usage is the ease with which it may be prepared. Ethyl alcohol can be produced by the fermentation of certain kinds of yeast by sugars appearing naturally in fruits, vegetables or grains. Fermentation stops when either all of the sugar is used up or when the concentration of alcohol in the liquid reaches about 15%. At this point the alcohol kills the yeast. Higher concentrations of alcohol can be achieved through the process of distillation in which the alcohol (which has a lower boiling point than water) is boiled off. Alcoholic beverages typically contain anywhere from 2.5% alcohol by volume (e.g. light beers) up to 40% alcohol (e.g. distilled spirits, vodka, rum).

ABSORPTION, DISTRIBUTION, EXCRETION

Alcohol is commonly taken orally as a beverage. Once swallowed it is absorbed rapidly from the gastro-intestinal tract including the stomach but especially from the upper intestine. Food in the stomach tends to lower the rate of stomach emptying and thus decreases the alcohol effect. Highly concentrated alcoholic beverages cause muscle spasms which retard stomach emptying and thereby decrease the rate of absorption.

Once absorbed, alcohol is distributed evenly throughout all body tissue and fluids including the brain. Because alcohol diffuses from blood into fat and muscle tissue, an obese or muscular person can drink more than a lean individual without becoming as intoxicated. Similarly, larger people, because they have greater volumes of blood in which alcohol can be distributed, can drink more without becoming intoxicated than can the smaller individual who has correspondingly less blood volume.

Once in the body, alcohol, unlike most other drugs, is broken down at a constant rate regardless of the concentration of alcohol in the blood. Thus, contrary to popular belief, there is nothing that one can do to speed up the rate of metabolism. Exercise, coffee, or other magical concoctions can *not* increase the rate with which the liver oxidizes alcohol to CO^2 and water. The average rate at which alcohol is metabolized is 10 ml. absolute alcohol per hour. This is roughly equivalent to 2/3's of a 12 oz. bottle of 5% beer, or 2/3's of a 1.5 oz. shot of rye whisky per hour. The rate varies somewhat from one individual to another depending upon body weight and liver weight (Goodman & Gilman, 1980).

Because the rate at which alcohol is metabolized is relatively slow and constant, any alcohol consumed in excess of the amount that can be metabolized accumulates in the blood. The amount of alcohol in blood at any one time is referred to as the blood alcohol level, or blood alcohol concentration (BAC). A BAC of .08% means that each 100 milliliters of blood contains 80 milligrams of absolute alcohol.

SHORT-TERM EFFECTS ON BEHAVIOR

Pharmacologically, alcohol is classed as a general depressant and is very similar in its effects to sedative hypnotic compounds such as the barbiturates (e.g. Nembutal and Seconal) and anti-anxiety agents such as Chlordiazepoxide (e.g. Librium) and Diazepam (Valium). Small amounts of alcohol produce relaxation and mild sedation. Larger amounts slow the electrical activity of the brain, inhibit dreaming (i.e. REM sleep), and depress respiration. At very high blood concentrations, depression of the central nervous system (CNS) may be so profound that death may result from respiratory arrest and cardiac failure.

It is widely held by the lay public that alcohol is a stimulant. Low doses of alcohol do have a mild stimulant effect on breathing, for example, but as the amount consumed increases, the general depressant effect also increases. Alcohol is thought to affect the organism in a progressive manner through a mechanism called inhibition (Goodman & Gilman, 1980). First to be affected are those centres of the brain which under normal circumstances control complex behavior and then, in a progressive manner, more basic functions are inhibited. Thus, control over motor functions becomes increasingly impaired so that, initially, fine motor functions and then gross motor functions including reaction time and eye-hand coordination become impaired. Thinking becomes disorganized; the drinker has difficulty in concentrating, memory becomes impaired, decision-making becomes increasingly difficult, and risk-taking increases.

This loss of inhibition of brain function is thought to be the cause of that spectrum of "drunken" behavior which characterizes intoxicated people. Large individual variations in drunken behavior occur in the moderately low to moderately high range of blood alcohol concentrations (.03-.25). Some individuals become extremely gregarious, confidence abounds, and their mood may be euphoric. Other individuals may become morose, withdrawn, and wide swings in mood and aggressive behavior may become evident. These individual differences appear to be related to a wide variety of factors including the drinker's mood before beginning drinking, the drinker's expectations, the setting, the extent of individual tolerance development, the behavior of others, and past learning experiences.

Generally speaking, under low to moderate degrees of intoxication, performance on a wide variety of tests involving concentration and vigilance and complex tasks which require attending to two tasks simultaneously is somewhat impaired (Moskowitz & Depry, 1968). In addition, studies have shown that performance is more impaired when BAC is rising than when it is falling. Thus, an individual will be more impaired at for example, .05% if BAC if rising than he will be at that identical BAC when his blood alcohol concentration is falling. Although objective measures reveal significant decrements in performance, speed and accuracy, drinkers tend to consistently over-estimate their performance, believing themselves to have performed better than they actually had. Similar errors in estimation of the degree of intoxication occur on the rising and falling aspects of BAC. Drinkers tend to over-estimate the degree of intoxication as BAC rises and under-estimate the actual falling BAC (Vogel-Sprott 1976).

LONG-TERM EFFECTS

Tolerance

Individuals vary greatly in the degree to which alcohol affects their behavior and in the severity of effects it has. These individual differences may result in part from congenital differences in initial tolerance or drug sensitivity. Thus, some individuals appear to have had a greater innate degree of alcohol tolerance on their first exposure to alcohol than others. However, major individual differences in the magnitude of alcohol effects are probably due primarily to the phenomenon of acquired tolerance. Tolerance may be defined as diminished effects of a given dose after repeated administrations such that less effect is produced by the same dose or conversely, such that the individual requires an increased amount of alcohol to attain the same degree of effect that he previously experienced with smaller doses.

Tolerance for alcohol can, in some individuals, reach extreme degrees. Some alcoholics can consume as much as three fifths of 80 proof liquor in one session of drinking without obvious signs of intoxication. Heavy users of alcohol can perform complex tasks at BAC's of .20, a blood level which would be associated with severe intoxication in a less experienced drinker (Talland, 1966; Talland & Kasschau, 1965; Talland, Mendelson & Ryback, 1964). It should be noted that some alcoholics may lose their tolerance for alcohol over time and become drunk after little more than one or two drinks.

Physical Dependence

When alcohol ingestion is abruptly stopped, a syndrome of effects, called "hangover" after a single heavy exposure, or "withdrawal" after prolonged heavy exposure is typically seen. Symptoms may include tremulousness, nausea, vomiting, anxiety, sweating, agitation, cramps and in rare cases, seizure, hallucinations and delirium tremens (DT's) may occur. Generaly speaking, the symptoms of withdrawal are opposite to acute drug effects. Thus, alcohol as a CNS depressant markedly reduces CNS activity; its abrupt withdrawal produces hyper-excitability of the nervous system. This phenomenon is called "physical dependence" and is said to have developed when the condition is reached in which the functioning of the nervous system is distressed when it is deprived of alcohol, i.e. when there is a physiological need for the drug for "normal" functioning. Physical dependence is indicated by the observation of withdrawal symptoms either upon abrupt cessation of drinking or when BAC drops. Other syptoms correlated with physical dependence are morning drinking and blackouts. Morning drinking is usually thought to occur when drinkers need to "self-medicate" with alcohol to reduce the severity of "morning after" effects such as tremulousness, nausea, and headache). Blackouts are total losses of memory for events occurring during periods of intoxication. Heavy drinkers may lose several hours or days of their lives and may fabricate stories to account for the forgotten time.

Current theories of drug tolerance tend to view tolerance and physical dependence as linked phenomena. Tolerance thus appears to develop only to those systems where the drug has reduced the capacity of the organism to function optimally (Kalant, 1971). Tolerance and physical dependence may be viewed as an adaptive response which enables the organism to adapt to what were, initally, debilitating drug effects.

Psychological Dependence

It has been customary in the alcoholism field to distinguish a second kind of dependence on alcohol from the physical dependence syndrome just described. This form of dependence has been termed "psychological dependence" and it refers to the development of a perceived need for alcohol on the part of the user for adequate functioning. Psychological dependence may be inferred when an individual regularly uses alcohol to deal with unpleasant emotional or physical states like tension, anxiety, depression and insomnia. An individual may be psychologically dependent on alcohol without consuming large quantities or becoming physically dependent.

ABUSE & ADDICTION

A major problem in the field of research and treatment of alcohol abuse has been the difficulty in defining when it is that someone who uses alcohol may be said to have a problem with alcohol. What behaviors distinguish the "alcoholic" or alcohol abuser from "normal" social drinkers? That question has preoccupied researchers for many years. Its answer requires a consideration of a controversy between two major theoretical camps: the so-called *medical model* of alcoholism and more recent *social learning* models.

According to the medical model, there is a disease entity called alcoholism characterized by loss of control over drinking of alcoholic beverages that is progressive and irreversible (Jellinek, 1960; Knott and Beard, 1966). Proponents of the medical or disease model have argued that the ultimate reason for the use of the "sick" or "diseased" label is to help channel resources to the alcoholic and thus to afford him that special care that society reserves for its ill (Getlow, 1973). Prior to the formal recognition by the World Health Organization of Alcoholism as a disease in 1975, abuse of alcohol was viewed as a moral weakness or a character flaw. The disease label offered the chronic alcohol abuser dignity and a right to therapy.

While the medical model is still accepted by many experts (Fox, 1967; Pendery, Maltzman & West, 1982), little empirical support for its assumptions of (a) total loss of control over drinking in diagnosed "alcoholics," or (b) progression, and irreversibility have been documented in the research literature. A number of studies have in fact, demonstrated that alcoholics rather than being totally unable to control their drinking can under certain circumstances actually moderate their drinking. This has been found in experimental studies both when the alcohol is consumed openly or surreptitiously (Engle and Williams, 1972; Merry, 1966; Sobell, Sobell and Christleman, 1972).

Similarly, with regard to the progressivity/irreversibility symptom, a number of studies have documented a return to "social," "normal" or "non-problem drinking" by previously diagnosed alcoholics (Anant, 1968; Davies, 1962; Bailey and Stewart, 1967; Kendell, 1965).

Social learning theorists argue that abusive drinking is a learned behavior which is maintained by a variety of antecedant and consequent events. Treatment is focussed on first identifying and then altering these maintaining factors so that the alcoholic may effectively modify or eliminate his abusive drinking behavior. They argue that such well-worn expressions as "First drink, then drunk" and "Once drunk, always a drunk" can act as dangerous self-fulling prophesies. They can serve to reassure the alcoholic that he is not responsible for controlling his own drinking behavior on those occasions on which he is not sufficiently highly motivated to do so.

Recently, documentation of remission in alcoholics (i.e. evidence that some former alcoholics can resume "normal" drinking) was presented in reports emanating from the Rand Corporation in 1968 and 1980 (Armor, Polich & Stambul, 1978; Polich, Armor & Braiker, 1980). These studies surveyed a large national sample of "alcoholics" treated at the National Institute on Alcohol Abuse and Alcoholism (NIAAA) treatment centers throughout the U.S. In the first (1976) study, 20% of clients were found to be drinking normally at an 18 month follow-up as compared to 25% who had been abstaining for six months or more, 205 who had abstained for 1-5 months, and 33% who were still drinking heavily. "Normal" drinking was intended by the investigators to mean "normative" levels of consumption and (as operationalized in the study) as drinking less than 3 oz. of ethanol per day in the past month, with no impairment of behavior or alcohol dependence symptoms.

The second (1980) Rand Report was a four year follow-up of the (1976) survey group. Methodologically the second report was superior to the first. It consisted of a much larger sample (N = 500), and a higher response rate, and it included more variables to assess alcohol-related impairment. Eighteen percent of treated "alcoholics" were found to be drinking without problems.

One of the most important findings of the Rand studies was that a cluster of three variables was found to differentiate those drinkers who were more successful in abstaining completely from alcohol from those who were able to drink in a non-problematic fashion. Marital status, level of alcohol dependence and age at the beginning of treatment were found to be highly related to prognosis:

> "For older persons with high levels of dependence at admission, long-term abstention at 18 months had a better prognosis (7% re-

> lapse) than did non-problem drinking (39% relapse). But the situation reverses for younger men with lower dependence, in which case non-problem drinking yields a better prognosis (5% relapse) than long-term abstention (24% relapse). For older men with low dependence or younger men with high dependence at admission, marital status plays the deciding role: Married men do better with long-term abstention (9% relapse) than with non-problem drinking (22% relapse), unmarried men do better with non-problem drinking (10% relapse) than with abstention (19% relapse)" (Armor, 1981, p. 342-3).

In summary, research has demonstrated that there are subgroups of individuals who have been labelled "alcoholic" who are able to significantly modify their drinking behavior for prolonged periods of time without resuming heavy drinking. These data are difficult to reconcile with a disease model of alcoholism.

In view of the foregoing evidence, it is curious why researchers and practitioners have continued in the heated debate about whether treatment methods should or must be directed to the goal of total abstinence for all patients. The debate actually appears to have intensified in the U.S. over the last few years. In part the persistence of the debate is attributable to the conceptual and emotional biases of practitioners some of whom are themselves recovered alcoholics. However, the differences of opinion cannot be entirely dismissed by such *ad hominem* considerations. One must bear in mind that many of the obstacles to resolving the debate arise from the major difficulties that are encountered in conducting adequate treatment outcome research which might address the issue. In this field, as we shall see, evaluation research is both technically and practically difficult. Many, perhaps most, of the studies whch might be expected to yield definitive answers to the question of controlled drinking versus abstinence are replete with methodological flaws. However, even definitive studies can be and have been criticized. We wonder whether any amount of data can ever resolve this debate which may be as emotional and political as it is scientific.

THE GOAL OF TREATMENT

The debate currently centres around the issue of appropriate treatment goals for alcohol-abusing clients. The work of the Sobell's (Sobell & Sobell, 1973) was highly influential in popularizing the concept of "controlled drinking" as an appropriate treatment goal in alcoholism treatment. The Sobells compared the effectiveness of individualized behavior therapy which had a treatment goal of controlled drinking, with a traditional abstinence-oriented alcoholism treatment method. They found that their controlled-drinking group functioned significantly better at 12 month follow-up than the comparison group on a variety of psycho-social indicators. Their results were subsequently confirmed in an independent follow-up investigation three years later (Caddy, Addington & Perkins, 1978).

Pendery et al. (1982) recently published a 10 year follow-up of the Sobell clients who had received individualized behavior therapy. Pendery et al. claimed that "a review of the official evidence, including official records and new interviews, reveals that most subjects trained to do controlled drinking failed from the outset to drink safely" (Pendery et al., 1982, p. 169). The apparent conflict between Pendery et al.'s conclusions and the Sobells' data contributed to major arguments throughout the addictions field not only about the reliability of research data but also about the question as to whether controlled drinking as a goal for alcohol abuse treatment is appropriate, reasonable or achievable.

Our comparison of the Sobells' original data with those reported in the Pendery paper reveals no significant discrepancies. Moreover, the Pendery et al. investigation contains major flaws in methodology and experimental design which seriously limit its value. For example, the investigators include no control group! They provide no follow-up data for traditionally treated clients but, instead, leave it to the reader to assume (correctly or incorrectly) that recovery rates in traditional programs are superior.

The conflict has been well publicized by the media and has had a significant effect on official policy in the treatment of addiction (Peele, 1983). Peele notes that "controlled drinking" is widely accepted as an appropriate treatment goal in the United Kingdom, but is not so viewed by treatment centres in the U.S.

> "This difference between the two countries in public policy is not the result of scientific inquiry. Rather, it reflects political forces and prejudices in America that forbid a reasonable discussion of the issues. The essential question is whether, in this atmosphere, we can find the best way to combat alcoholism" (Peele, 1983, p. 42).

THE PARADIGM SHIFT IN THE ALCOHOLISM FIELD

In summary, many researchers have shifted in their conceptualization of "alcoholism." Former views of "alcoholism" as an all-or-none dichotomous disease entity have been replaced by the concept of "problem drinking behavior." There is a growing acceptance of the dimensional nature of alcohol abuse: problem drinking is viewed as a behavior lying on a continuum from abstinence (no drinking) to continuous heavy drinking. Drinking behavior, in turn, often leads to problems in other aspects of social, vocational, psychological or health functioning.

This shift in conceptualization is reflected, for example, in the recently revised Diagnostic and Statistical Manual (DSM III) of the American Psychiatric Association (1980). In DSM III, diagnoses related to the use or abuse of alcohol appear primarily in the "Substance Abuse Disorders" section under the major topic "Alcohol Dependence." Two diagnoses are possible: "Alcohol Abuse" and "Alcohol Dependence." Alcohol dependence may be diagnosed when alcohol has (a) impaired social or occupational functioning *or* (b) when the pattern of its use is considered pathological *and* when (c) either tolerance or withdrawal can be documented. Alcohol abuse, on the other hand, may be diagnosed when, in addition to (a) and (b), a duration of disturbance of at least one month can be documented.

An even more important development in the alcoholism field which reflects this paradigm shift is reflected in the World Health Organization Task Force Report (Edwards, Gross, Keller, Moser, 1977). This report identified an *Alcohol Dependence Syndrome* which includes the following symptoms: increased tolerance to alcohol, personal awareness of a compulsion to drink excessively; the repeated occurence of withdrawal symptoms; and intermittent periods of abstinence followed by re-establishment of the syndrome. This core dependence syndrome is distinguished from *alcohol-related disabilities.* The latter includes any physical' psychological and social problems resulting directly or indirectly from excessive drinking. The most important feature of the WHO system as compared to the DSM III diagnostic system is the recognition of quantitative variations among individuals. Thus, both the "alcohol dependence syndrome" and "alcohol-related disabilities" are seen as dimensions of behavior rather than all-or-none states.

CAUSES AND CURES

It is probably reasonable to suggest that there have been almost as many suggested causes of alcoholism as there have been individuals who have studied the phenomenon. It may also be fair to say that there are as many causes of alcoholism as there are individuals who exhibit the problem.

It is important to note that very few people (including offenders) become "alcoholic" according to the classical definition of the "GAMMA ALCOHOLIC." Gamma alcoholics include those individuals who are unable to stop drinking once they have begun. Such individuals often evidence periods of abstinence interspersed with periodic binge drinking. Their loss of control is confined to the single drinking session because a gamma alcoholic can abstain, i.e. choose not to start drinking on a given occasion. Increased tolerance, physical dependence and serious physical and social problems are also usually evident. Only about 5-7% of North American males would qualify as "alcoholic" given this definition (Polich et al., 1981).

As we are all aware, however, many individuals experience serious problems related to their drinking without evidence of marked physical dependence on alcohol. Cahalan (1970) has estimated that up to 36% of the population could be considered to have a drinking problem.

It is safe to say that anyone who drinks alcohol is at risk for developing an alcohol problem. Simply increasing the frequency of drinking can result in the development of tolerance and physical dependence. This risk is probably enhanced if alcohol is used as a coping response for dealing with psychological or social problems such as shyness, anger, frustration, tension or anxiety. Thus individuals who feel that they are not much fun at a party unless they have had several drinks, or who use alcohol to relax after a stressful day, may easily become psychologically dependent on alcohol.

Why some individuals progress from psychological dependence to daily excessive drinking while others do not is not well understood.

> "Large scale national and regional epidemiological surveys of drinking practice which have followed, over a long period of time, individuals with varying degrees of social problems, have shown that people move in and out of symptomatic drinking, that the severity of drinking problems may remain constant and non-progressive and that remissions and progressions vary significantly over time, place and circumstances" (Pattison, 1982, p. 6).

Various authors suggest that personality factors in combination with unique life stresses at particular phases in the life cycle are highly related to the development and cessation of drinking problems in a given individual. The multivariate factors operating in the development of problem drinking suggests that no one treatment is likely to be the treatment-of-choice for all cases. There are no "across-the-board" treatments; no elixirs; no panaceas.

CHAPTER 6

ALCOHOL ABUSE PROGRAMS FOR NON-OFFENDERS

BEFORE discussing the efficacy of alcohol abuse programs for offenders in correctional settings, we wish to examine the status of alcoholism treatment programs in general. At first glance, the evidence for the efficacy of treatment for alcoholic *non*-offenders is impressive. However, the long standing controversy about the effectiveness of correctional treatment (the "nothing works" debate) has a parallel in the literature on the treatment of alcoholism. On the one hand there are those who conclude that alcohol abuse treatment, in most cases, is followed by improvement. For example, Poley, Lea & Vine (1979) concluded that after one year of treatment, 40% of the clients in a typical program would be successfully treated or well on their way to a successful outcome, and that 70% of the clients would be noticeably improved.

Emrick's (1974) analysis of 265 evaluation studies found an improvement rate of two-thirds. In their national study of a large number of treatment programs in the U.S., Armor, Polich & Stambul (1978) found that there was

> ". . . substantial improvement on a number of outcome indices. The relative rate of improvement for males is about 70% for those outcomes most closely tied to the alcoholism syndrome, such as consumption and behavioral impairment" (Armor et al., 1978, p. 152).

On the other hand, there are less sanguine reviewers who reach quite the opposite conclusions:

> "In spite of a vast amount of research into many different treatment approaches, there is no evidence from recent studies to suggest that treatment favourably alters the outcome of alcoholism . . . from what is known about the outcome of non-treatment, there is evidence which suggests that even the most effective programs may only marginally improve on the success rate of non-treatment" (Rix, 1977, p. 137).

Hill & Blane's (1976) analysis concluded that post-treatment improvement rates were less than 50%. Similarly, on the basis of a review of 384 alcoholism treatment studies, Emrick (1975) concluded that in the majority of cases "significant results were short-term, due to chance or not directly related to life adjustment." Costello, Bechtel & Giffen (1973) reported an average "improvement" rate at one year of only 21% for 33 follow-up studies which included 8,393 cases. In a more recent review, Clare (1977) concluded that

> ". . . there is little evidence that costly and intensive therapeutic interventions are more efficacious than more economic and simpler approaches in bringing about remission. The case in favour or the significant effects of treatment in alcohol addiction remains to be conclusively established."

Failure to find differences between different treatment modalities has also been reported by Emrick (1975), Ruggels et al. (1975), and Armor et al. (1978), leading the latter to suggest that "the fact of treatment is more important than the method." Baekeland, Lundwall & Kissin (1975) wondered "whether we should applaud the treatment programs or the patients they treat," and Belasco (1971) suggested that "elaborate treatments may be not better than brief, sensible advice."

Armor et al.'s review (1978) indicates that outcome depends less on the kind or amount of treatment than on the client's alcohol history and social background. Treatment variables explain only a little of the variation in remission rates. This means, perhaps, that the major factor in alcoholism remission may be the client's decision to enter treatment.

> ". . . over and over we were impressed with the dominant role the patient as opposed to the kind of treatment used on him

played both in his persistence in treatment and his eventual outcome" (Baekeland, Lundwall & Kissin, 1975).

A common assertion in program studies is that "our program only works with those who stay with the program or those who are motivated to change" (Sobell, Sobell & Ward, 1980).

In large measure, the controversy about treatment efficacy stems from the penchant of reviewers to make summary generalizations which are not justified, given the quality of the research on which they are based. There have been several large scale evaluations which have attempted to assess the overall efficacy of alcoholism treatment by aggregating data from a number of treatment programs or studies (e.g. Armor, Polich & Stambul, 1978; Baekeland, 1975; Emrick, 1975; Ruggles et al., 1975; Towle, Bosely, Borgeson, Gray, Mothershead & Norwood, 1973; Polich, Armor & Braiker, 1981). These across-the-board evaluations and reviews have met with many of the same criticisms which were directed at Martinson's (1974) general condemnation of correctional treatment programs. Martinson's "almost nothing works" conclusion was also based on a across-the-board, aggregate assessment of a large number of programs.

The individual programs on which the summative reviews of alcoholism treatment success are based have used different methods, lengths and intensity of treatment, different measures of outcome, and various populations of subjects with different drinking histories and personal characteristics. Given the complexity of the interactions between outcome, treatment (type, intensity, duration), setting, and client characteristics, any *general* conclusions about the efficacy of alcoholism treatment are likely to be unwarranted and misleading.

Even the small-scale evaluation studies on which the aggregate reviews are based are typically plagued with methodological shortcomings (Maisto & Cooper, 1980). These may include a failure to control for spontaneous remission or decrease in drinking with age; failure to consider the biasing effect of selecting only those treatment candidates with favorable prognosis; failure to specify population characteristics; failure to study the characteristics of addicts who refuse to enter treatment or drop out early; and including only program completers in program assessment. A major shortcoming is the failure to employ standardized, well validated, and reliable outcome measures of drinking behavior or social adjustment. Perhaps the factor which most limits the conclusions of these studies vis-à-vis the effects of treatment is limited information about the course of alcoholism *without treatment* (Polich et al., 1981). Remission with or without treatment may be quite high, although Smart's (1975) review calls this area of research into question.

Tempering the pessimism about the potential of treatment of the addictions are the conclusions of Miller's (1980) recent comprehensive reviews of outcome investigations which found that in short-term follow-up about one-third of those treated become abstinent; one-third are "improved"; and one-third remain unchanged or deteriorated. Although long-term follow-up shows somewhat lower rates, these rates of improvement following treatment compare favorably to average recovery rates without treatment (about 19%) (Miller 1980). Moreover there are several recent well controlled and carefully evaluated studies which have demonstrated the effectiveness of *some* forms of treatment with *some* alcoholics (e.g. Azrin, 1976; Hunt & Azrin, 1973; Sobell & Sobell, 1973, 1976).

More important are those studies which have demonstrated that treatment outcome depends upon the characteristics of the clients treated. For example, the outcome of alcoholism programs has been shown to be related to the client's social stability (employment, residence, family relationships) (e.g. Rosenblatt et al., 1971); socio-economic class (e.g. Trice et al, 1969); and history and duration of alcoholism (e.g. Vogler, Weissback, Compton & Martin, 1977). In fact, some studies have found that pretreatment subject characteristics can account for about 70% of the variance in treatment outcome (Vogler et al., 1977).

TREATMENT GOALS

It is important to note that the view that total abstinence is the only hope for the alcoholic and the only adequate measure of program outcome has been convincingly challenged. Following treatment, long-term abstinence is relatively rare even at short-term follow-up (Emrick, 1974). However, there is considerable evidence that many former problem-drinkers become, or can learn to become, controlled drinkers. They can drink moderately without becoming seriously impaired (Armor et al., 1978; Lloyd & Salzberg, 1975; Pattison, 1976; Polich et al., 1981; Pomerlau & Adkins, 1980; Smart, 1975). Even without treatment, some former alcoholics have become controlled drinkers (Davies, 1962).

These findings are important not only for outcome evaluation in corrections but for client motivation. Advising an alcohol-involved offender that he must never drink again can be a decided turn-off from program acceptance. Interestingly, flexible goal setting appears to be less appropriate for older chronic alcoholics than for younger problem-drinkers. The correctional population probably includes many more of the latter.

It is also important to keep in mind that the achievement of controlled drinking (or even total abstinence) does not necessarily imply improvement in general social adjustment. Evaluation of programs should, but seldom does, include measures of both alcohol consumption and social and legal behavior.

CHAPTER 7

ALCOHOL ABUSE PROGRAMS FOR OFFENDERS

IT cannot be assumed that the conclusion of evaluators regarding the efficacy of alcohol treatment in general are appropriate to offenders. Many program studies, particularly those which are provided in community settings, include both offender and non-offender subjects. However, it is not possible to determine whether the foregoing conclusions are applicable to the treatment of individuals who have alcohol-related problems and are also offenders since it is rare that research reports indicate whether or not their clients are offenders. There is some evidence to suggest that offenders and non-offenders who have alcohol-related problems may differ significantly in terms of factors such as social class which may be related to program outcome (Ross, 1971). Polich et al. (1981) have noted that alcoholic felons are likely to have *less* serious social and personal problems than clinic-treated alcoholics even though they may have the same symptoms in terms of alcohol abuse. However, the extent to which correctional populations differ from clinic populations is simply not well enough understood to warrant generalization of the findings from general alcohol treatment programs to correctional populations or to correctional settings.

Although there are a few reviews of correctional alcohol treatment programs provided in the literature, they are limited to surveys of the various programs which have been provided in various jurisdictions (Goodrick, Vigdal & Sutton, 1976; Roffman & Froland, 1976; Thomas, 1978). Surveys fail to reveal much about the quality of programs. They also tend to concentrate exclusively on programs in institutions and fail to describe the availability of services in community correctional settings such as probation, half-way houses, or community residential centres. None have critically reviewed the available evidence for the *effectiveness* of correctional programs.

Data from a 1974 LEAA survey of 10,400 inmates in 190 U.S. state prisons indicated that 22% of the inmates were judged to require alcohol rehabilitation. However, only one in four (25%) of such inmates actually participated in such programs.[11] Roffman & Froland's (1976) review indicated that surveys of state institutions in the U.S. revealed that prison programs either do not exist or are superficial and that the level of treatment response is by no means commensurate with the problem (Frank, Mooney & Pavloff, 1973). A survey of state prisons in the U.S. found that 70% of "habitually very heavy drinkers" had never been in an alcohol treatment program (Kalish, 1983). A 1978 survey of U.S. Federal prisons concluded "while promising treatment approaches have emerged in recent years, they have not yet been utilized to any appreciable degree in correctional facilities" (Thomas, 1978, p. 4).

Our search of the 1970-80 literature revealed a large number of individual reports on alcohol treatment programs in correctional settings. Given the many rather negative assessments of reviews of the efficacy of treatment of alcoholics in the general population, and the prevalent "nothing works" view of correctional treatment in general, one might be less than optimistic for treatment programs for alcohol-related offenders. However, there is some evidence that *some* programs may benefit *some* offenders.

ALCOHOLICS ANONYMOUS

The surveys clearly reveal that the most common correctional response to the treatment needs of alcohol-related offenders is the provision of AA programs (Correctional Service, Canada, 1981; Thomas, 1978; Wells, 1973).

It is the rare prison that has no AA program. Prison AA programs may well have value beyond providing a leisure-time activity, or social support, or (in settings where it is allowed), a means of maintaining some contact with visitors from the community. AA may also have value in terms of prison adjustment. Roth & Rosenberg (1971) evaluated the value of AA in terms of prison adjustment. Three groups of inmates in a medium security penitentiary were compared: fifty inmates with a chronic history of alcohol abuse who were attending AA; fifty not attending AA; and a control group of fifty with no history of alcohol-abuse. Alcohol abusers attending AA evidenced significantly better insitutional behavior (staff ratings and participation in vocational training programs) than alcohol abusers who did not attend AA. It is not possible to determine whether the better adjustment was a result of AA or whether those who attended AA were inmates who would have adjusted better no matter what program was provided.

There is some suggestive evidence that AA programs in prisons may contribute to improvements in recidivism. AA appears to be a component part of almost every multi-facetted alcohol-abuse treatment program in correctional institutions which has reported positive outcome results. However, in no case is it possible to determine the relative contribution of AA to such programs. For example, in 10 of the 18 camps which comprise the Mississippi State Penitentiary at Parchman, inmates are provided with group and individual therapy when they participate in AA. Contingent on their participation for at least six months they also receive post-release job placements and are provided with a volunteer sponsor or "big brother" to assist them in the community. The results of this program have been very encouraging: over a three-year period only 4.6% of program participants (parolees and dischargees) have returned for any reason, whereas 30% of the inmate population as a whole have been returned for parole violation alone. This is a major difference, but studies which much improved methodology are required to determine whether these results are attributable to the program or to the AA componenet or simply reflect that the inmates who had the motivation to attend AA for six months were better prospects for rehabilitation in the first place!

The same problem is encountered in attempting to judge the reports of success of AA in community correctional settings. For example, extraordinary success was reported for the AA programs in four half-way houses in Houston, Texas (Wells, 1973). Less than 5% of 561 multi-recidivistic offenders had to be returned to prison during the first three and one-half years of operation. New York State's PACT program claims a 40% success rate for 6,000 offenders in achieving complete sobriety in a one-year follow-up. The program offers offenders a choice between a jail sentence or fine and treatment in a sub-acute detoxification unit which offers primarily an AA program (Ball & Weiss, 1976). The Hazelden Rehabilitation Center in Minnesota which provides a program based on AA has reported that 50% of a group of 288 court-referred offenders were abstinent for twelve months after treatment (Laundergan, Spicer & Kammeier, 1971).

None of the foregoing studies employed an evaluation methodology which would justify confidence in their claims of success. None provided any data for untreated groups, and none provided baseline or pre-post data on either drinking or illegal behavior. Claims of success in obtaining abstinence were based on unsubstantiated client testimonials which were probably highly suspect since failure in many cases might lead to return to court and possibly a jail sentence. One study even used self-report of criminal acts to support their claim of 90% success in reducing arrests (Laundergan et al., 1979). One might wonder why any offender would volunteer information on his criminal acts to a clinic which had close ties to a court!

Pallone & Tirman (1978) found that among 469 clients with alcohol problems (43% court-referred), those who attended AA and the regular therapy program had significantly higher remission rates than those who did not attend AA. The investigators failed to consider the possibility that these results may only reflect that those who chose to attend AA were better prospects for remission with or without AA.

Tempering the positive reports of the effects of AA is a study which found that only 24% of chronic public inebriates improved in terms of drinking behavior and social functioning in an 8-month follow-up of 165 cases who were involved in an AA program in a mental health center (Costello, Giffen, Schneider, Edgington & Manders, 1976). However, judging programs to be failures is just as inappropriate as judging them to be effective when their evaluation methodology is inadequate, as it was in this study.

Selection artifacts such as the motivation of program joiners are also a confounding variable in research on the effects of AA with non-offenders. For example, the Rand nationwide study of alcoholism treatment in the U.S. found that regular AA attendance was almost as effective (56% remission) as a large variety of clinic treatment programs (63% – 72% remission) (Armor et al., 1978). However, it was simply not possible to determine whether these results were program effects or simply indicate that individuals who intended to modify their drinking are likely to attend AA. Supporting the motivational interpretation, it was found that irregular AA attenders had much lower remission rates. It should also be noted that for the alcoholic who does not attend AA, a high amount of clinic treatment increases remission rates considerably (as much as 28%). Even for regular AA attenders the addition of clinic treatment substantially adds to their chances for remission. In sum, an AA program *may* be beneficial alone, but its effectiveness will likely be enhanced by the addtion of other program components. Further research is required before it can be determined whether these conclusions can be generalized to corrections.

One concern which must be expressed regarding AA relates to the goal of total abstention. If abstention is the measure of treatment efficacy, then AA may fare better than most programs. The Rand study found that "the regular AA participant is about 20% more likely to be a long-term abstainer than is a non-AA client" (Armor et al., 1978, p. 120). However, as noted earlier, the total abstinence goal of AA or any other program may be highly discouraging (and unrealistic) for many offenders, particularly younger ones whose alcohol-related problems are not chronic. That the imposition of unrealistic success criteria can be a major determinant of program failure is indicated in Fry & Miller's (1976) study of the abject failure of a community skid row clinic program which provided AA and other services to chronic alcoholics including many court-referred subjects. The initial goal for these chronic alcoholics was ninety days working without drinking; a goal which was rarely achieved. The unrealistic goal adversely affected not only the patients but also the staff. Staff morale was seriously jeopardized and they began to concentrate on control rather than treatment. The unrealistic goals, added to several organizational conflicts, led to the program's failure. Flexible goal setting may be essential for alcohol programs.

Many correctional workers assert that AA programs are the best programs and, perhaps, the only programs that correctional agencies need to provide for alcohol-abusing offenders. To be sure, they are the cheapest and the easiest to implement; they require no high-priced professional staff, a relative minimum of institutional planning and supervision; and, as a self-help activity, they avoid the stigma of psychiatric care which many offenders find abhorrent.

Recent evidence, however, suggests that enthusiasm for AA should be tempered. Research indicates that AA programs may be effective for a particular sub-group of alcohol abusers, but it may have, at best, no effect and, at worst, harmful effects for others (Ogborne & Barnet, 1982; Miller, 1980; Brandsma, Maultsby & Welsh, 1980).

Table 1 summarizes a large number of variables which have been found to be associated with successful AA affiliation. Although some of the variables listed have to date received somewhat limited empirical scrutiny, it is becoming increasingly clear that AA may be quite inappropriate for individuals who possess few of these characteristics.

Table 1

CHARACTERISTICS ASSOCIATED WITH SUCCESSFUL AA AFFILIATION

PERSONALITY VARIABLES:	1. External Locus of Control
	2. High Affiliation Needs
	3. High Dependency Needs
	4. High Authoritarianism
	5. Conformist
SOCIO-ECONOMIC VARIABLES:	1. High Education
	2. Middle-Class
	3. Male
	4. Age above 40
PSYCHO–PATHOLOGY:	Low Psychopathology
ALCOHOL DEPENDENCE:	High; Binge Drinking, Loss of Control
PERCEPTUAL STYLE:	Field Dependent
COGNITIVE STYLE:	1. Low Conceptual Level
	2. Cognitive Simplicty
TREATMENT HISTORY:	Frequent Hospitalizations
RELIGIOUS ORIENTATION:	High Existential Concerns

Some of the factors listed in Table 1 may characterize many offenders (e.g. external locus of control, dependency, authoritarianism, field-dependence, low conceptual level, and cognitive simplicity (Ross & Fabiano, 1985). However, in other respects the data in Table 1 raise serious doubts about the value of AA for offenders. AA affiliators who are likely to be successful come from middle to upper-class backgrounds, have high education, low psychopathology, high existential concerns, and are over the age of 40. These characteristics are likely to be found only in a small proportion of the correctional population.

> "Not only the emphasis on the 'comback' underlines middle-class American values, but the verbal skills and 'talking' therapy that are central to AA also are more compatible with middle-or-upper-class background. Furthermore, greater motivation for successful AA affiliation may be found in middle-class alcohol addicts since their alcohol-related behaviour has generated a greater degree of deviance from role expectations than is the case in lower status addicts" (Trice & Roman, 1970).

PHARMACOTHERAPY

Many claims have been made for the efficacy of treating alcoholics with a wide range of drugs (tranquilizers, phenothiazines, lithium, barbiturates, paraldehyde, antidepressants, LSD).[12] Although some drugs may be helpful in controlling anxiety or depression or other symptoms which may accompany problem drinking (and which may maintin the desire for alcohol), claims for their value in influencing drinking behavior are based on very questionable evidence (Armor et al., 1978; Benor & Ditman, 1967; Mottin, 1973).[13] Moreover, in the case of some drugs, a number of side-effects, potential long-term damage, and the possibility of engendering substitute addition, may outweigh the potential benefits of the drug (Schuckit, 1980).

Some early experimental and quasi-experimental studies with *non*-offender clients provided some support for disulfiram (Antabuse) (Gerard & Saenger, 1966; Wallerstein, 1957; Hoffs, 1961). However, there is considerable controversy about the value of disulfiram or other aversively protective agents. Antabuse may be a value adjunctive treatment (Costello, 1977; Hunt & Azrin, 1973). It may serve as a short-term crutch or as a "chemical fence" for those who are strongly motivated to stop drinking (Baekland et al., 1971), or as a means of keeping the client dry while other treatments are being provided. Its effectiveness depends on the duration and regularity with which it is taken. In other words, its effectiveness depends on the client's motivation. Side effects (drowsiness, headache, nausea, body odor, etc.) or extended usage may decrease motivaton for its use and contraindicate its prescription for clients who have medical problems such as cardiovascular disorder, epilepsy, or cirrhosis.

Antabuse is a common component in multi-facetted correctional programs but we found no study of its relative value in such programs. Moreover, we found no controlled evaluation of the value of Antabuse alone as a treatment in correctional settings. Routine prescription of Antabuse to alcohol-related offenders is unlikely to be effective (or safe) since the client must be motivated to take the pills and to accept total abstinence as his goal. The practice in some correctional jurisdictions of making Antabuse treatment mandatory (Haines, 1978) may have appeal to deterrence advocates but it is not based on empirical evidence of its efficacy.

INDIVIDUAL PSYCHOTHERAPY AND COUNSELLING

Scott (1977) has described his "success' with psychotherapy in case studies of five released inmates, but there are no adequate evaluation studies of psychodynamically oriented psychotherapy in correctional alcohol treatment.[14] Reviews of the effects of psychotherapy with alcoholics in general have concluded that there is very little evidence for its efficacy (Armor et al., 1978; Hayman, 1956; Hill & Blane, 1967; Voegtlin & Lemere, 1942).

Individual counselling is a component of most multifacetted correctional programs (e.g. Kennedy, 1980). However, in most instances, counselling takes a behavioral rather than a psychodynamic approach, deals with here-and-now issues and tends to be supportive or confrontational. No study was found which examined the relative effects of such services or compared the outcome associated with different approaches. Many correctional institutions have hired full or part-time alcohol counsellors (e.g. Cahill, 1978). Their impact has not been systematically examined.

GROUP THERAPY

Group therapy programs are among the most popular of correctional alcohol programs. Unfortunately, their popularity is not matched by evidence of their efficacy. Whereas some programs have claimed success (e.g. Scott, Keener & Manaugh, 1977; Collier & Somfay, 1974) most of the evidence for such success consists of anecdotal data, unsubstantiated and global recidivism data, or personal testimony by the clients (or by the program director!). For example, Scott (1976) "estimated" that he saw "about 500 convicts" in group therapy in an Oregon penitentiary who were on a work release program. He concluded that "although the work is difficult and demanding, he results offset the hardships of the task." The "results" he referred to were a "success" rate of 55%. We must add that this was the rate for the centre in which the program was provided, not just for those who were treated!

Group therapy is frequently a component in multi-facetted programs which have reported success with alcohol-related offenders. For example, Pallone & Tirman (1978) reported that total remission was observed at treatment termination in 67% of 314 clients in a multi-facetted program which included group counselling. The authors failed to assess how many of the clients who received group counselling (28% of the total) had a successful outcome! In no studies of the outcome of multi-facetted programs was the specific effect of group therapy studied, nor have the effects of group therapy been compared systematically with those of other treatment modalities.

One program which has been more adequately evaluated provides only some tentative support for group therapy in alcohol programs for offenders in community settings. Costello, Bechtel & Griffen (1973) conducted one of the few prospective studies in the literature. They obtained baseline data with careful assessment of outcome including one-day breath probes, reports from collateral informants, study of court, jail, and hospital records, and independent judgements of status. A one-year follow-up revealed that 33% of 100 cases consisting of chronic "revolving-door" alcoholics from local jails were "successful" (stringently defined) compared with a baseline success estimate of only 18%. This was a significant result although the percentage of successful cases was low. However, as is too common in alcohol treatment research, a substantial proportion (26%) of the subjects could not be located for follow-up. This makes the interpretation of the results highly questionable since these may have included many program failures. Unfortunately, the particular contribution of group therapy cannot be ascertained since the 30 day program included a host of other techniques including physical reconditioning, aversive conditioning, AA, and electrosleep.

Our search identified only one adequately controlled study of group counselling for alcohol-related offenders in a correctional institution setting. The results of the experimental study are not encouraging. One hundred and fifty inmate volunteers with a history of excessive use of alcohol were randomly assigned to either of two eight-week group therapy programs or to a control group receiving routine institutional care. Therapy consisted of small "awareness groups" with "confrontation," "rap" sessions, recreational activities, didactic presentations, community excursions, and discussions with individuals from the community. No significant benefits were found for the treated subjects relative to controls on several personality measures, post-release employment, arrest histories, alcohol consumption, attendance at AA, or one-year recidivism rates (Annis, 1979).

There is really very little reason to expect that group awareness, confrontation, and rap sessions, etc., will have much effect. Group therapy was touted as a correctional panacea in the sixties but recent reviews have found that the results of studies of the efficacy of group therapy for offenders in general have been far from supportive (Julian & Kilman, 1979; McCord, 1977; Ross, Currie & Krug-McKay, 1980). The outcome of group therapy for non-offender alcoholics has also been marginal (Baekeland, et al., 1975; Armor, et al., 1978). Accordingly, it should not be surprising that there is little evidence for the efficacy of group therapy with alcohol-related offenders.

It must be pointed out that the terms "group therapy" or "group counselling" refer to a remarkably wide variety of group intervention techniques. The terms no longer have any clear referent and general statements about their efficacy have little utility. It is reasonable, however, to assert that in our search no group therapy program based on a psychodynamic model was identified which has been demonstrated to be effective in an adequate evaluation with alcohol-related offenders. This does not imply that group programs in general are ineffective. In fact, most alcohol-abuse programs in the general population which seemed to "work" were conducted on a group basis or in a therapeutic community (e.g. Mrad & Krasnoff, 1976). The contribution of the group process to outcome variance in correctional programs has not been established, but Costello's (1977) review of 113 *non*-offender alcohol-abuse programs indicated that a therapeutic community was an essential factor in success.

Group therapy also has the potential for detrimental effects. For example, an additional analysis of the data from Annis's experimental study described above revealed that although no main effect of treatment was found, the recidivism of some types of offenders (those low in self-esteem) was *higher* following group therapy than following regular institutional care without specific alcohol treatment (Annis & Chan, 1983). Annis also found that the recidivism for some offenders (those with high self-esteem) was lower following group therapy than following regular institutional care. These results demonstrate that in the case of alcohol programs, just as in the case of any other correctional program, differential treatment effects should be expected; some offenders will do better, some worse. The advisability of matching treatment to patient is apparent. We will discuss this matter more fully in Chapter 8.

REALITY THERAPY

Probably the most widely acclaimed and most seldom evaluated program for offenders is reality therapy. Several reports on multimodal correctional alcohol treatment programs indicated that reality therapy was included in their program package but its relative contribution to program outcome has not been evaluated. A vivid description of the apparent advantages and shortcomings of reality therapy in an adult institution is provided in the report of the STAR program (Steps Toward Alcohol Rehabilitation), but no evaluation has been provided (Berlinger, 1973).

Pallone & Tirman (1978) reported total remission of 67% for 314 clients (41% court-referred) who were treated in a program which provided reality therapy in either individual and group sessions, or both. They also reported partial remission in 12% and "no significant change" in only 20.6% of the treated clients. To conclude that these outcome data indicate success for a reality therapy program would be somewhat generous given that they provide information about drinking behavior only at treatment completion, not at a later point. Moreover, clients who received reality therapy in individual sessions were *less* likely to attain remission than those who did not receive such services.

The efficacy of reality therapy with correctional clients remains to be convincingly demonstrated.

TRANSACTIONAL ANALYSIS

Only one study was found which assessed the value of transactional analysis (TA) with alcohol-abusing offenders (Ziegler, Costello & Horvat, 1976; Ziegler & Kohutek, 1978). This is surprising in view of the continuing popularity of TA with other correctional populations.

Ziegler et al.'s claims of positive effects of TA in their multi-modal prison program are questionable given the inadequate quality of their program evaluation. They reported that 80% of those returned to the community were "doing well" and had no subsequent convictions in a two-year follow-up. They neglected to define "doing well" and failed to provide a control group.

Although the potential of TA in an institutional setting for young offenders has been demonstrated in a well designed study by Jesness (1975), its value with offenders with alcohol-related problems has yet to be established. Mrad & Krasnoff (1976) have noted that dropouts are frequent in TA programs for alcohol-related offenders.

However, in terms of dropping out, TA programs are not an exception (Rubington, 1970). Ziegler, (1976) has presented a transactional analysis model of alcoholism and its treatment, but convincing evidence of its value is lacking.

HYPNOSIS

Paterson (1974) has suggested that hypnosis has value as an adjunct to other programs for alcoholic offenders. However, he bases his assertion only on case studies of three prison inmates. Hypnosis generally appears, for a variety of reasons, to be very rarely used with offenders. Our search revealed no evaluation studies of hypnosis in correctional settings, or of related techniques such as autogenic training, although Paterson (1974) claims these techniques have been used in prisons in a number of countries.

MARITAL AND FAMILY THERAPY

Family factors play a major role in the development and maintenance of drinking problems and in their treatment (Bromet & Moos, 1977; Cadogan, 1973; van Dijk & van Kijk-Koffeman, 1973; Orford, Guthrie, Nicholls, Oppenheimer, Egert & Hensman, 1975). Alcohol abuse in a family member can engender considerable stress in other family members. Problem-drinking may serve to maintain a pathological family system (Armor et al., 1978). On the other hand, higher levels of family cohesion and lower levels of conflict may be related to the maintenance of abstinence among serious problem drinkers. When marital cohesion and support is high, treatment may be effective but it is unlikely to be so when cohesion is low (Finney, Moos & Newborn, 1980; Orford, Oppenheimer, Egert, Hensman & Guthrie, 1976; Moos, Bromet, Tsu & Moos, 1979). Accordingly, family and marital therapy have often been recommended as a treatment or as an adjunct to treatment for alcoholics.

Although there are some clinical reports of success with family therapy with alcoholism (Corder, Corder & Laidlaw, 1972; Esser, 1970; Smith, 1969), there are few controlled empirical evaluations in which family therapy was the central componenet of the program. On the other hand, some studies have found that the addition of family therapy can contribute significantly to a multi-facetted program (e.g. Corder et al., 1972; Hedberg & Campbell, 1974; Hunt & Azrin, 1973). One study found that behavioral family counselling based on Stuart's (1969) and Patterson & Reid's (1973) model was the most effective of four treatment programs in the treatment of alcoholics in a mental health center (Hedberg & Campbell, 1974).

It is regrettable that there are only a few reports which indicate that family therapy has been used with alcohol-related offenders in correctional settings. It is more regrettable that there is a dearth of empirical evaluations of such programs particularly in view of the fact that the value of involving family members in the treatment of adolescent offenders has been demonstrated in a number of well evaluated programs (Alexander & Parsons, 1973; Alexander, Barton, Schiaro & Parsons, 1976; Maskin, 1976; Arnold, Levine & Patterson, 1975; Eyeberg & Johnson, 1974; Johnson, 1977; Kent & O'Leary, 1976; Wade, Morton, Lind & Ferris, 1977).

COGNITIVE TRAINING

A common component of correctional programs which have been found to be effective in reducing the recidivism of offenders is an intervention strategy which enhances the offender's *cognitive* development, improves his problem-solving skills, and teaches him more effective interpersonal reasoning strategies (Ross & Fabiano, 1981; 1985). Such programs have led to reductions in recidivism ranging from 30-60% in follow-up studies as long as 3 to 15 years after treatment. Various cognitive techniques have been used, including self-control training; problem-solving and interpersonal skills training; negotiation skills training; and modelling and role-playing.

There is some evidence that a cognitively oriented program may also have value for offenders with alcohol-related problems. Cox (1979) has described a program for incarcerated alcoholic offenders which is based on Maultsby's (1971, 1974) rational behavior training program, a highly directive method of teaching reasoning skills. Eighty adult male felons with histories of chronic alcohol abuse were reported to have reduced their number of discipline infractions in the institution from 26 per month to 6 per month after 3 months of programming. During a 6-month follow-up only 13% of the participants (N=15) had problems severe enough to warrant parole revocation. All of the participants had been recidivists prior to participation.

Rational behavior training was also employed in Ziegler & Kohutek's (1978) multi-modal program for 79 penitentiary inmates who had a history of drinking-related crimes and an average of four prior incarcerations. Many had been flagrant rule violators prior to program entry but during the six-month program the participants committed no major disciplinary infractions. In a 2-year follow-up, 80% were found to be adjusting well in the community.

The absence of data on untreated comparison groups and other methodological shortcoming of these studies limit their value. However, their results and the evidence of the effectiveness of similar programs with other offenders suggests that cognitive programs merit further study.

Cognitive factors play an important part in the development of problem-drinking (Marlatt, 1978). Moreover, following treatment, the individual's cognitive reaction to a relapse may be a crucial determinant of his continued drinking (Marlatt, 1978). Many offenders who experience a relapse some time after completion of an alcohol treatment program view any occasion of "falling off the wagon" as testimony of their inability to control their drinking. They interpret relapse not simply as a temporary set-back but as total failure which proves that they never will be able to stop drinking. Such reasoning represents cognitive errors, (e.g. overgeneralizing, catastrophizing) which may be inappropriate, unreasonable, and self-defeating. By attributing too much significance to what may be an isolated event the individual may perceive himself as helpless and totally controlled by alcohol. Such thinking, in turn, can lead him into giving up his resolve to control his drinking.

It has been suggested that involving an offender in cognitive training during treatment could help him to avoid attributing subsequent relapses to personal inadequacies and to help him recognize how his inappropriate and extreme assessment of his behavior and its significance can have unfavourable consequences for him. He needs to learn to recognize the effects of temporary situational stresses and to appreciate that one drink does not make a drunk.

Unfortunately, few studies have been made of the cognitive functions of *offenders* with alcohol-related problems. In correctional programs emphasis has more commonly been on studying psychodynamics. No evidence was found of effective correctional treatment derived from a psychodynamic explanation of alcoholism. Perhaps programs derived from cognitive models might prove more valuable. We will discuss this possibility more fully in the final chapter. Interestingly, a recent study found that the inclusion of a cognitive training component in general correctional treatment programs significantly differentiated effective from ineffective programs (Ross & Fabiano, 1982; 1985).

BEHAVIORAL PROGRAMS

With the exception of a few descriptions of individual case studies (Cohen, Leibson, Faillace & Speers, 1971; Pickens, Bigelow & Griffith, 1973), there are remarkably few reports of behavioral programs for alcohol-related offenders in corrections and even fewer evaluation studies.

Contingency Contracting

Behavioral contracting using such things as release dates as rewards has been used as a method of motivating offenders to attend alcohol programs and to maintain sobriety (Berlinger, 1973; McGrath, O'Brien & Liftik, 1977; Sielaff, 1977) but most programs have not been evaluated except with very small samples (Miller, 1975a). Miller (1975b) has suggested that half-way houses should establish contingencies between breathalyzer tests of blood alcohol concentration and the availability of services such as food, shelter, or counselling. Such a program was found to decrease the number of public drunkenness arrests and increase the number of days employed in a group of skid-row alcoholics. No changes were found in a control group receiving services on a non-contingent basis. The witholding of basic services presents major ethical (and legal) problems. Whether or not the contingent application of non-essential services or rewards (e.g. cigarettes) may provide sufficient potency, has not yet been examined with correctional populations with alcohol-related problems. However, we can report that contingency contracting is an integral component of many effective correctional treatment programs. This may augur well for its use in correctional alcohol-abuse programs.

Systematic Desensitization

Systematic desensitization does not appear to have been used extensively with alcoholics in corrections in spite of some success this approach has had with alcoholics elsewhere in decreasing anxiety and physiological disturbances which may be engendered by the absence of alcohol, or in decreasing anxiety in interpersonal situations which might heighten the need for alcohol (e.g. Hedberg & Campbell, 1974).

Relaxation Training

Goodrick et al. (1976) and Kennedy (1980) employed relaxation training in their prison alcohol programs in attempting to teach offenders how to relax instead of drink, but no evaluation of this approach has been reported.

Aversive Conditioning

Since the early enthusiasm stemming from Shadel's (1944) study which found a 60% remission rate with an aversion program, a number of aversion programs have been reported. Such programs have yielded a wide range of abstinence rates (30% to 90%) (Armor et al., 1978). Unfortunately, in general, the quality of evaluation has been unsatisfactory and reasonably high remission rates are usually found only with short-term follow-ups. Even with periodic reconditioning "booster" sessions (which may be essential), aversive conditioning has little support unless it is accompanied by other therapies which can teach the patient alternative behaviors. Curtailing problem drinking *may* be essential, but it does not appear to be sufficient. One must not only extinguish former maladaptive behaviors but teach alternative prosocial adaptive behaviors.

Although a recent experimental study (Boland, Mellor & Revusky, 1978) found positive results, the value of using aversive conditioning *alone* in treating alcoholics in the general population has been seriously questioned (Miller, 1976; Nathan, 1976; Baekeland et al., 1975). The application of this technique (particularly in corrections) raises difficult ethical/legal issues. However, it has been used as one component in some effective multi-facetted behavioral programs.

Broad-Spectrum Behavioral Programs

Multi-modal behavioral programs which include a variety of behavioral techniques may have considerable potential for offenders with alcohol-related problems. Vogler, Weissbach & Compton (1977) compared the relative effectiveness of two different multimodal behavioral treatments for 80 alcoholics ad problem-drinkers including many referred by the courts. Treatment was either "wet" (consumption of alcohol was required) or "dry." "Wet" techniques included videotape feedback of the client's behavior while under the influence of alcohol, blood alcohol concentration (BAC) discrimination training to teach the recognition of levels of intoxication, aversion training to teach awareness of cues associated with intoxication, and avoidance training. "Dry" techniques included alcohol education, behavioral counselling, social skills training, contingency contracting, and training in alternative behaviors incompatible with drinking. Booster training was provided for one year. No significant differences were found between "wet" and "dry" treatments, but overall, 63% of the subjects were classified as either abstinent or controlled drinkers at a 12-month follow-up. Unfortunately, in the absence of outcome for an untreated control group, it is not possible to determine the value of what appear to be impressive results.

The success of multi-facetted behavioral programs with the general correctional population (non-alcohol related) suggests that such programs should be extended to offenders with alcohol-related problems (Ross & Gendreau, 1980). Too often practitioners have become enamoured with a particular therapeutic modality (typically, one which is "in vogue") and in their treatment efforts, slavishly adhere to that program for better or worse, excluding all others, till failure do them part! Such unilateral approaches do not do justice to the complexity of criminal behavior and their failure is predictable. Its failure in such unrealistic projects often leads to a widespread disenchantment with the technique which, though it may have little value by itself, may have considerable potential when used in combination with other techniques.

In another well-controlled multi-facetted behavioral study, Hunt & Azrin (1973) trained relatives and friends of alcoholic patients to provide pleasurable social activities only when the patient was sober. The patient's intoxication resulted in a loss of these reinforcers. Vocational counseling, job placement, a buddy system (a non-alcoholic social club), marital and family counselling, and Antabuse were also provided. Treatment subjects fared significantly better than a control group receiving routine hospital care not only in terms of drinking frequency, but also in terms of institutionalization, and employment.

Some comparative studies have found better oucomes for multimodel behavioral programs for alcoholism than for traditional therapies (e.g. Pomerleau & Adkins, 1980). However, no adequately controlled studies of multi-facetted behavioral programs with alcohol-abusing offenders appear to have been conducted, and no other reports were found of *correctional* alcohol programs which employed behavioral programs such as social skills training, cognitive behavior modification, BAC discrimination training, coping skills training, cue exposure training, or self-control training. Vogler et al's (1977) results with alcohol-abusing offenders, and the success of multi-modal behavioral programs in the treatment of other offenders and in the treatment of the general population of alcohol abusers, indicates that their value in correctional alcohol treatment programs should be explored.

MULTI-MODAL PROGRAMS

In the foregoing section we discussed multi-facetted programs in which the components were primarily behavioral techniques. There are also multi-modal programs in which the component techniques comprise a broader range of therapeutic modalities but are not limited to behavioral approaches (e.g. Gay, 1973; Kennedy, 1980). Some claim what appear to be exceptional results. A two-year follow-up of Ziegler & Kohutek's (1978) program which combined transactional analysis, rational self-counselling, biofeedback training, confrontation and encounter groups reported that 80% of those returned to the community were doing well and had not been returned to custody. Of the 20% judged as "failures" almost half were returned to prison for "technical" violations of their parole rather than for committing new crimes. A number of weaknesses are evident in this study not the least of which is the absence of a statement on the exact number of subjects released to the community. The term "technical violation" is never defined and may well include the abuse of alcohol. Finally the authors fail to point out how they defined or verified the "acceptable behavior" of the majority of their clients.

Coffler & Hadley (1973) reported that a 90-day program which provided occupational and recreational therapy, individual and group psychotherapy, and counselling was associated with a significant reduction in the number of drunkenness arrests for 713 court-referred men arrested for public intoxication. The average number of arrests for public intoxication in a 12-month post-treatment follow-up was 4.2 compared to 8 in the year preceding treatment. The investigators failed to provide information regarding the arrest rate for non-treated offenders. The same problem is found in Pratt's (1975) study which found a 51% abstinence rate among 274 skid row alcoholics three months following their treatment in a multi-facetted program which was offered in lieu of a jail term.

Although multi-facetted alcohol programs are common in corrections, only a few have been evaluated and they have been evaluated poorly.

DRIVING WHILE IMPAIRED PROGRAMS

The majority of driving while impared (DWI) programs include lectures and films designed to emphasize the gravity of alcohol-related driving offences, classes on the effects of alcohol on driving skills, lectures on the physiological, behavioral and social effects of alcohol consumption, and discussions on motivational factors in drinking and the law as it relates to alcohol use. Many are provided as part of a probation order and, therefore probation supervison must be considered as an integral part of the treatment. The court's decision to order probation, possibly as an alternative to incarceration, the restrictions on the offender's freedom (including driver's license suspension), and the requirement to "keep the peace" must also be considered part of the "treatment." In some instances the program is provided directly by the probation staff; in others through referral to other agencies which may provide additional services such as antabuse, psychotherapy, and AA.

Our search revealed a plethora of reports on DWI programs few of which provided adequate information regarding their effectiveness (Hayslips, Kapusinski, Darbes & Zeh, 1976; Scoles & Fine, 1977). Landstreet (1977) has described in detail many of the planning, organization, and management aspect of such programs and emphasized the necessity of adequate evaluation but has reported no outcome data for the programs he describes. Most DWI evaluations have used unsophisticated methods. Most studies have been limited to pre-post tests of knowledge or attitude change. These factors may or may not be related either to subsequent drinking behavior or to criminal behavior.

Some studies have reported a very low incidence of post-treatment DWI offences. For example, Hall (1977) reported a 3% recidivism rate, and Walter (1975) a 4% repeater rate for driving under the influence of alcohol and a 3% rate for reckless driving. Clay & Swenson (1977), Malfetti & Simon (1974) and Pollack (1973) also reported that recidivism rates were reduced by DWI programs. However, it is important to note that the recidivism rates were often so low in the first place that the DWI-associated reduction in recidivism must be viewed as unsubstantial (Armor et al., 1978). Moreover, in the absence of adequate non-treated controls, the low recidivism rates could in no case be attributed to the program.

Not all DWI programs have reported success. Zelhart's (1973) study found *no* reduction in recidivism although those who completed the program (the best motivated clients?) had significantly fewer accidents and fewer non-alcohol-related offences following the program.

The best designed evaluation studies of DWI programs appear to yield the most unfavorable results. Thus, a quasi-experimental study which compared four counties which had implemented a DWI program for first offenders and four which had not, found that program participants had the *worst* subsequent accident and conviction records. The program had no advantage over mandatory licensing controls. Scoles & Fine (1977) conducted an experimental study which examined alcohol consumption (rate and amount) by 122 DWI first offenders. Subjects were randomly assigned to either a DWI educational program or a no-treatment control group. A 30-day follow-up revealed *no* significant benefits for the treated groups. A 30-day follow-up may not be sufficient to assess the outcomes of such programs. It must be noted that the educational program in this study was not intensive. It consisted of four weeks of two-hour classes, two classes per week. Though perhaps not much different from the norm for DWI programs, it would seem unduly optimistic to expect major benefits from such a limited program effort.

Holden's (1983) evaluation of the Tennessee DWI probation project was also impressive. The program was not; neither was the outcome. The study involved a large sample: 4,126 persons arrested for drunk-driving in Memphis. The research design provided random assignment to treatment conditions: probation supervision with alcohol education and therapy (assertiveness training); probation supervision without education and therapy; education and therapy without probation supervision. A randomly assigned no-treatment control group was also provided. The study also was impressive in that it differentiated between social drinkers and problem drinkers and provided a two-year follow-up after referral to the project. It was found that the programs were *not* effective in terms of rearrests for DWI or misdemeanors and felonies. It is to Holden's credit that he notes that, "the treatment programs were just too weak to have any effects on recidivism . . . were short term and were not very intensive" (p. 68). He also notes that "the programs clearly were inappropriate for a large proportion of the project's clients" and that "the education and therapy programs seem to have been designed for a clientele which largely did not exist" (p. 68).

One might wonder why Holden would provide such an elegant evaluation for such a lack-lustre program. It is commendable that he did so; the Memphis program may not be very different from the vast majority of DWI programs in expecting great profits from small investments! We urge caution, however, in endorsing Holden's conclusions about the ineffectiveness of rehabilitative programs for drunk driving offenders. As Sechrest (1979) has pointed out the fact that research has not established the efficacy of rehabilitation programs does not mean that we can with assurety conclude that such programs are ineffective. We are puzzled by the confidence that some social scientists have in proving the null hypothesis! Surely we should be careful in rejecting all programs, regardless of their quality, based on the apparent failure of poor programs which never should have been expected to work in the first place.

The results of a recent study would, at first glance, demand that we temper our remarks about the differences in outcome between weak programs and intensive programs. Swenson & Clay (1980) addressed the question of treatment intensity in DWI programs. Using a follow-up period of 8 months they compared outcome for 314 subjects randomly assigned to either a 10-hour DWI educational program, a 15-hour educational program plus group confrontation/personal awareness sessions, or a home-study course which involved only a single 30-minute session in which participants were provided with educational material for home study. Outcome was measured in terms of responses to a questionnaire re. drinking behavior (quantity and frequency), employment stability; physical health; and social adjustment. *No* difference were found between the different programs; the minimally intensive program was just as effective as the others. Remission was nearly 70% for each program in spite of the fact that the home study "program" was much cheaper.

Thus it would appear that success through DWI programs might be achieved at minimal cost and with minimal program investment. However, it must be noted that this study included no untreated control group. Attributing the 70% remission rate to the program cannot be justified in view of the limitations in the evaluation methodology. Moreover, DWI participants are often social drinkers who may be unlikely to evidence further drinking-related problems whether or not they receive treatment. Furthermore, high DWI remission rates may reflect not treatment effects but a deterrent effect form being arrested and convicted (Scoles & Fine, 1977).

Further research needs to be conducted comparing DWI program outcome with social drinkers and problem drinkers to determine whether they have different treatment needs and whether the social drinkers require minimal treatment . . . or no treatment at all. Related to this question, Meck & Baither (1980) found that, at least in the case of DWI programs, there are important differences between offenders 26 and older and those 25 and younger. The latter group appear to require some kind of therapeutic program and not only DWI.

Programs for DWI offenders must carefully screen clients at intake and provide them with treatments which vary both in intensity and the degree of clinical intervention depending on the nature of the client's problems. Thus, social drinkers may require only educational programs whereas problem drinkers may require education plus many other services. Saunders & Pemberton's (1979) program permitted such tailoring. They found that subsequent accidents and DWI offences were lower for participants than for a matched control group which was not referred to the program. Unfortunately, the matching of the groups did not exclude the possibility of selection bias.

Holden's (1983) study of the Memphis DWI project also included matching procedures but his failed to yield differential treatment effects. However, as we noted in Chapter 4, effective programs must be multi-facetted, intensive, and must be appropriate to the problems of the offenders they are designed to effect. It is not surprising, therefore, that the Memphis program did not reduce the post-treatment criminal behavior of its clients. As Holden (1983) points out, "many of the project's clients appeared to drive while drunk as part of a general pattern of criminal deviance . . . (and) programs aimed solely at modifying drinking and driving behaviors are not likely to be effective for such individuals" (p. 68). Holden's remarks should be remembered in evaluating other DWI projects.

ALCOHOL EDUCATION

Many correctional settings offer alcohol education programs which are similar to those used in DWI programs but are designed for offenders with alcohol-related problems which are not limited to driving while impaired (e.g. Goodrick et al., 1976; Kennedy, 1980; Pratt, 1975). These programs are often provided in conjunction with other program services (e.g. life-skills; pre-release preparation). An educational component is often a mainstay of such programs.[15]

Educational programs may be more attractive to offenders than clinical programs since they are less likely to make them feel they are being identified as individuals with psychological problems. Moreover, they may "break the ice" and serve as a way of "seducing" a reluctant or poorly motivated offender into other treatment programs which he might otherwise reject.

Alcohol education programs may be very useful adjuncts to other programs but they also may have important benefits on their own. Some offenders may simply not be aware of the complex effects that alcohol consumption can have on their percepton, their emotions or their behavior. Many are unaware of the effects of varying amounts or kinds of alcohol or of the interactions between their physical and psychological state and the effects of alcohol. Educational programs may help them achieve an understanding of how to minimize the potentially damaging effects of alcohol and to modify their consumption and its effects. One's beliefs about alcohol's effects can have a strong influence on behavior; one that is independent of alcohol's physiological effects (Lang, Goeckner, Adesso & Marlatt, 1975).

Some educational programs (particularly those which include confrontational techniques) may help by making the offender realize or accept the fact that he has a drinking problem (e.g. McGrath et al., 1977). This may be an *essential* step in successful treatment.

Alcohol education programs in corrections are common and in many cases their rationale seems reasonable. However, we found no evaluation which would enable a determination of whether, by themselves, the suffice to effect changed behavior. Moreover, we found no assessment of their relative contribution as components in a total treatment package. Their value is strongly suggested, but not proven by Walter's (1975) study which found a recidivism rate of only 4% for subsequent driving offences among 802 DWI offenders in a probation alcohol education program.

We shall discuss alcohol education programs further in Chapter 8. There is a possibility that particular forms of educational programs *may* have particular value for *some* offenders.

DETOXICATION

Detoxication centers were designed to decriminalize public intoxication, prevent the revolving-door incarceration of chronic drunken offenders, and reduce the costs and overcrowding of courts and jails which are associated with a criminal justice approach to such individuals. They provide public inebriates with temporary lodging and acute medical care. There were also rationalized as a means of integrating individuals with alcohol-related problems into the health-care system rather than into the criminal justice system. This was to be achieved by referring detoxication center clients to rehabilitation services for longer-term inpatient or outpatient treatment following their brief stay in the detoxication center.

There has been very little evaluation of their success in achieving such goals. There is some evidence to indicate that the detoxication approach can reduce the number of public drunkenness arrests and the time and money spent by the criminal justice system in handling these offenders (Sacramento, 1974). However, it appears that detoxication centers are by no means achieving all of their goals. Hamilton's (1979) quasi-experimental study which examined 52 chronic drunken offenders who received detoxication and referral services and 48 comparison subjects, found that the detoxication clients improved in their self-reported quality of life and appeared to be in better physical health over a one-year follow-up. Nevertheless, there was *no* benefit associated with detoxication care in terms of the number of subsequent episodes of drunkenness although detoxication clients had longer periods of abstinence.

Annis & Smart (1978) found that over a 6-month follow-up, almost half of 522 detoxication clients were arrested (three or four times in 25% of the cases) and more than half of the men were readmitted to detoxication centers (20% of them at least three times).

"The predominant pattern was multiple involvement with police, detoxication, residential and outpatient facilities." This study seems to indicate that detoxication centers are failing in terms of their goals of rehabilitation. However, the study failed to assess what the outcome would have been in the offenders had been processed through the criminal justice system rather than through detoxication and the social welfare system.

Further doubts on the rehabilitative potential of detoxication centers are raised by the results of a quasi-experimental study which compared patients who were referred to and received post-detoxication treatment and those who did not (Smart, Finney & Funston, 1977). *No* significant differences in subsequent detoxication admissions or criminal convictions were found.

The apparent failure of detoxication to affect rehabilitation may reflect not the impotence of alcohol treatment *per se,* but the failure of the system to ensure that such treatment is actually provided. Detoxication centers were intended to divert the chronic drunkenness offender from the criminal justice system into the health-care system where treatment could be provided. It is becoming apparent that a simple referral approach is ineffective. Annis & Smart (1978) found that of all admissions for detoxication in their study (N = 1202), only 9.6% ever arrived at the agencies to which they were referred! Smart et al. (1977) found that 38% of a group of 114 detoxication patients refused to accept a treatment referral for post-detoxication care. Only 40% of those who accepted a referral actually arrived. Ninmer (1971) found that although 75% of detoxification patients volunteered for further care, only 30% actually used the rehabilitation service provided.

The problem is not only one of getting detoxication clients into treatment. It is also one of keeping them there. The "no-stay" rate may be as high as the 'no-show" rate. Annis & Smart (1978) found that 80% of detoxication clients who actually arrived at the referred service dropped out of treatment by the fifth appointment.

Detoxication centers may even be failing to achieve their purpose of getting the chronic drunkenness offender out of the criminal justice system and into the health-care system. Annis & Smart's (1978) study found that among their sample of 1202 detoxication clients, those who were arrested for drunkenness following their detoxication experience were processed by the criminal justice system rather than being readmitted to a detoxication center.

The foregoing underlines the importance in alcohol treatment of specifying what goals a program has, ensuring that services and practices are related to these goals and evaluating the program vis-à-vis these goals and not only vis-à-vis goals which the program is not intended to achieve. In the area of detoxication, it appears that realistic goals are not rehabilitative ones but social and economic ones: getting drunks off the street; providing them with medical care; redefining drunkeness as a medical/social welfare problem rather than as a criminal justice problem; reducing overcrowding of jails and courts; and reducing housing, policing, court, and corrections costs. Improved screening procedures may lead to improved cost-effectiveness of the medical services provided by enabling quick identification of serious medical problems and providing expensive medical services only for those who really require them (Feldman, Pattison & Sobel, 1975).

Finally we should note that although detoxication centers may be achieving a few of their purposes they may also be "creating their own revolving door" (Smart et al., 1977). However, in our opinion, their revolving door may be better than that which characterized the criminal justice system approach to the chronic drunkenness offender. Jails should be reserved for criminal offenders who require secure custody.

PROBLEMS, ISSUES, AND CONCLUSIONS

Surveys of several correctional jurisdictions have indicated that the number of treatment programs for offenders with alcohol-related problems, the quality of such programs and the variety of services they provide are insufficient given the extent and complexity of the alcohol/crime link and the prevalence of alcohol problems in the correctional population. However, there are correctional alcohol treatment programs which appear to be comprehensive in scope, systematically planned and implemented, and conceptually sound. Many are multi-facetted programs which provide an impressive array of services.

Many programs report successful results in terms of improvement in drinking behavior and many report extremely low post-treatment recidivism rates. Unfortunately, the efficacy of most program efforts has not been adequately assessed. Almost none of the programs have been properly evaluated; most have not been evaluated at all. The claims of success are rather generous, and possibly extravagant, given the inadequate methodology on which these claims are based.

Some programs have been "evaluated," but their evaluation is limited to such things as counting the number of clients, determining how long the program has been continued, and discussing how inter-agency cooperation can be achieved (e.g. Cahill, 1979). Assessment of whether programs have some benefit for their clients are much less common. Ironically, in spite of the interest in studying the administrative efficiency of these programs, almost no study has been made of cost-benefits . . . or money wasted.

The low quantity of outcome evaluation studies is matched by their poor quality. Most studies are characterized by an impressive array of methodological shortcomings. Most fail to provide base-rate data or information on outcome rates for non-treated clients and we are left to guess whether the "success" of treated clients is attributable to the program or simply to the passage of time. This should be a major concern for correctional evaluators particularly in view of Goodwin et al's (1971) study which found a 40% remission rate among 223 alcoholic male felons after 8 years. When data are presented for untreated groups there is usually a failure to demonstrate (or determine) their comparability to the treated groups. One is left to wonder whether the best prospects are treated and the worst are not. Claims which are made for treatment effects may only be selection artifacts. Experimental studies with random assignment of subjects to treatment and non-treatment groups are rare. Quasi-experimental studies are generally of poor quality. Few studies have compared the relative effects of different treatments administered to comparable groups of offenders.

The measures of outcome in many studies have often been crude, inadequately validated, and insensitive. Many studies simply report the percentage of clients "improved" without indicating what "improved" means or how it was determined. Typically, outcome reports rely on the offender's self-report of his drinking behavior without checks on the accuracy of these reports. "While the *overall* reliability and validity of the self-reports of alcohol abusers have been found to be satisfactory for most purposes, discrepancies do occur" (Sobell & Sobell, 1980, p. 178). One likely discrepancy is with offenders for whom honest self-reporting may have adverse legal consequences.

Most correctional research has limited its assessment of alcohol program outcome to measuring (however crudely) post-treatment alcohol use. It has not been determined what relationship there is between improvements in drinking behavior and social/legal adjustment. Although a few studies have found that alcohol use is associated with recidivism, it seems to have been taken for granted, without further study, that if an offender reduces the frequency of his drinking he will have a higher likelihood of rehabilitation. Abstinence or controlled drinking cannot be equated with rehabilitation (or vice versa). It is necessary to measure more than just drinking behavior.

A major shortcoming of many studies was their failure to consider client attrition in assessing treatment outcome. Drop-out rates from alcohol programs are usually very high and "shrinking samples" are common. Few correctional studies appear to have been sensitive to this problem. Many report outcome data only for program completers who may have been those with the most favorable prognosis in the first place. They fail to report how many of their clients are drop-outs (these may have had the worst outcome).

CHAPTER 8

DEVELOPING ALCOHOL ABUSE PROGRAMS FOR OFFENDERS

OUR search failed to identify specific alcohol treatment programs for which there is convincing evidence of success with offenders either in community correctional settings or in institutions. There are simply not enough studies with adequate methodology to justify any firm conclusions about the benefits (or the failure) of correctional alcohol-treatment in general or about the relative effectiveness of particular treatment modalities or combinations of treatment modalities. However, a consideration of the correctional alcohol treatment literature in the light of research on correctional treatment in general, and in the light of research on alcohol-treatment in the broader (*non*-offender) population, does lead to some tentative conclusions on a number of important issues.

WHY TREAT?

Given the limitations in our understanding about effective alcohol abuse treatment generally, how can we proceed to develop programs specifically for offender populations? An even more basic question may be, *Should* we develop treatment programs for offenders at all? For several reasons our response to that question is a strong affirmative.

First, although it cannot be stated conclusively that alcohol and drug abuse *cause* crime, there is certainly an abundance of evidence which suggests that criminal behavior is highly related to alcohol abuse. The correlation could, of course, be the result of a direct relationship between alcohol use and the commission of illegal acts, or it might simply reflect the effect of a third "causal" variable such as deficits in behavioral and/or cognitive competencies. Alternatively, the observed relationship with criminal behavior may be a result of a more complex interaction between deficits in behavioral/cognitive competence and alcohol abuse such that the disinhibiting effect of alcohol is more profound on an individual with "low competence" than on an individual who has more effective coping skills. Clearly, further research is required before definitive answers to these complex questions can be obtained (Collins, 1981).

Second, we do know from several reviews of the alcoholism treatment literature with *non*-offender populations that *some* treatment programs have a substantial impact on drinking behavior for *some* clients. On average, in short-term (6-12 months) follow-up investigations, about one-third of those treated become abstinent; one-third are "improved"; one-third remain unchanged and/or deteriorated (Miller, 1980; Emrick, 1975). Although long-term follow-up usually reveals somewhat lower rates, these rates of improvement following treatment compare favorably to average "spontaneous remission" rates (i.e. recovery without treatment) of about 19% (Miller, 1980).

The most fundamental concern of society and of correctional administration and program staff, however, is with the potential impact of effective addictions treatment not only on drinking behavior but also on the probability of future illegal behavior. In other words, the pivotal question from a corrections perspective is the relationship between addictions treatment and recidivism. Clear demonstrations of the impact of addictions treatment on offender recidivism would provide strong support from a "cost-effectiveness" perspective for the implementation of offender addictions treatment programs. Such information cannot be gathered, however, until adequate offender addictions treatment programs are implemented and subjected to compehensive evaluation. Thus, a third rationale for the provision of addictions treatment is the need to develop a broad data base from which to assess treatment efficacy particularly with reference to offender recidivism.

The fourth rationale is essentially a moral justification. There is convincing evidence that the prevalence of alcohol abuse among offenders is very high. Regardless of the relationship between alcohol use and crime, alcohol abuse can engender many physical, emotional, behavioral and social problems for such offenders, and for their spouses, their families and, most important, for those who are victims of their behavior.

HOW TO TREAT?

Given that we agree that addictions treatment should be provided to offenders, the next question to be addressed is what type or types of treatment programs should be developed.

Our review suggests that in the main two types of offender programs have been in vogue; AA groups and educational programs. Both kinds of programs have probably been broadly instituted for a number of pragmatic and political reasons rather than on the basis of a careful assessment of offenders' program needs. AA programs are, for example, extremely inexpensive requiring a minimum of institutional planning and supervision and no professionally trained staff for their implementation. Similarly, educational programs are far more attractive to many offenders than is a "therapeutic program" in that they may involve themselves in such a program without necessarily indicating that they personally have an addictions problem. Some educational programs have the added advantage of providing an opportunity for inmates to earn academic credits as part of an upgrading program. Quite aside from these efficiency issues, however, is the question of whether or not such programs are most likely to be effective in changing addictive behaviors for the majority of the alcohol abusing offender population.

As our review indicated, the efficacy of AA, either alone or in combination with other program modalities, has yet to be demonstrated with offender clients. Positive outcomes may say more about the motivation of participants who join and continue in AA than about the actual benefits of the program itself. This does not mean that it should not be provided; it only suggests that optimism for its effects cannot yet be justified. Moreover, enthusiasm for AA should be tempered by the results of recent research which indicates that although AA programs may be effective for a particular subgroup of alcohol abusers, it may in fact have at best no effect, and at worst harmful effects for others (Ogborne & Barnet, 1982; Miller, 1980; Brandsma et al., 1980). The particular abusers for whom it is most likely to be effective are those who are least likely to be found in the correctional population: well-educated, middle or upper class individuals who have high existential concerns, low psychopathology and are over 40 years of age.

Educational programs, like AA, are a popular form of offender addictions treatment. Typically, these programs are based on the premise that providing information about alcohol and its effects will lead to changes in drinking behavior. The empirical literature seems to indicate that acquisition of factual information may change attitudes, but it is questionable whether it changes behavior.

Kalb (1975) has identified five factors which influence behavior change following provision of factual information:

a) the potential severity of the negative consequences of continuing in the behavior,
b) whether the effects of the behavior on the individual are immediate or delayed,
c) the believability of the espousing authority; the educator,
d) the degree of immediate primary and secondary reward value (pay off) that the behavior provides,
f) the degree of availability of alternative behaviors that can produce the same rewards for the individual.

Kalb (1975) argues that campaigns designed to point out the dangers of a particular behavior such as alcohol abuse run the risk of damaging the credibility of both the message givers (alcoholism authorities) and the message itself (alcohol/drug facts). This is particularly the case when the probability of negative consequences is low as it is in the criminal justice system where detection, apprehension, and conviction are relatively rare events.

We might also be pessimistic about the gains which will accrue from providing information on the adverse consequences of alcohol abuse to offenders who, in large number, seldom consider the consequences of their behavior (Ross & Fabiano, 1981). Educational "warnings" may be necessary but not sufficient.

> "The situation is exactly what happens in attempts to inform the public on the 'dangers of marijuana.' The public feels that these statements are false on the basis of comparing what they are being told with what they have previously experienced or know through the experience of friends. This approach has resulted in a wide credibility gap between the proselytizers and the users. What remains, therefore, is that not only do many people (including the alcoholic population) behave in a manner that seems to disregard available facts about the dangers of alcohol, but the 'facts' themselves are frequently looked upon with suspicion" (Kalb, 1975, p. 409).

As we indicated in our review, there has been very little controlled evaluation of alcohol education programs in corrections. Such programs may be helpful in sensitizing offenders to the possible harmful effects of alcohol and may, because they are "nonclinical," serve as a means of getting offenders involved in more intensive programs. They may be a useful, even a necessary adjunct to treatment but there is little reason to suppose that in the absence of other program components they will have significant impact on the offender's behavior.

We must emphasize that our doubts about the efficacy of alcohol educational programs should not be taken as a rejection of educational approaches to offender rehabilitation. On the contrary, most of the correctional programs which have been demonstrated to be effective are educational in nature (Ross, 1982). However, they do not simply provide information, they teach social skills, problem-solving skills, and thinking and reasoning skills (Ross & Fabiano, 1983, Vol. 2). Alcohol education programs which include such components may be particularly valuable for offenders with alcohol-related problems (Ross & Fabiano. 1985).

Another problem with alcohol education programs should be noted. A recent review of addictions educational programs (Kinder, Pope & Walfish, 1980) indicted that they may actually *increase* the frequency of use and may yield a shift in attitude towards experimental use of "softer drugs." Clearly then, some caution should be exercised in the development and implementation of alcohol educational programs, given that attitude and behavior change in the opposite to intended direction may occur. The proliferation of alcohol education programs for offenders, particularly young offenders does not appear to be justified by empirical research.

FUTURE DIRECTIONS

If the two most popular kinds of offender addiction programs seem unlikely to be effective (by themselves) with the offender population and if, as our review indicated, none of the correctional programs which seem to have promise have been adequately evaluated, what can we recommend to correctional managers and practitioners? What kind of interventions are most likely to be effective? In order to address this question we need to go beyond the *correctional* literature on alcohol treatment.

The treatment of alcoholism in non-correctional settings appears to be in a state of transition. Previously popular program models are being seriously questioned and innovative program practices are being developed which are based on current knowledge of alcohol — its use and abuse. These developments are rarely reflected in the literature on alcohol-abuse treatment in corrections. Alcohol-abuse programs for offenders are not characterized by innovation and the correctional alcohol literature does not reflect a self-critical stance. Most programs appear to be based on old, staid, and untested conceptualizations of alcoholism. An assessment needs to be made of the programs currently in place and those being contemplated to determine whether their conceptualization is in accord with developments in our understanding of alcohol and its abuse.

We found *no* evidence of the efficacy of therapies based on a medical (disease) model of alcoholism or crime, but the available evidence attesting to the effectiveness of programs derived from any other model was tenuous at best. However, analysis of effective correctional programs for the general offender population clearly indicated that effective programs were based not on psychodynamic models but social learning or cognitive models (Gendreau & Ross, 1979). Most effective programs sought to improve skills (cognitive, interpersonal, vocational) and attitudes rather than attempting to cure some presumed underlying illness or psychopathological condition.

Disenchantment with medical models also seems to characterize the general alcoholism literature. Recent program efforts in the general field are based on an understanding of alcohol-abuse as a complex problem which involves physiological, emotional, behavioral, cognitive, attitudinal, social, and cultural factors. Accordingly, *multi-facetted* programs have become popular. Several carefully evaluated comprehensive programs, based on social-learning theory and employing multi-facetted behavioral techniques, have yielded impressive results with alcoholics and problem-drinkers (Azrin, 1976; Hunt & Azrin, 1973; Sobell & Sobell, 1973). The effectiveness of such programs, and of other programs based on social-learning models, should be examined in controlled trials with offenders with alcohol-related problems. Support for this suggestion is provided by studies which have found that behavioral programs with controlled drinking as the goal have proven superior to traditional programs (Nathan & Briddel, 1977; Pomerlau & Adkins, 1980). Sobell & Sobell (1973) found that their broad-spectrum behavioral program yielded success rates of 80% and 75% (abstinence and controlled drinking, respectively) compared to 33% and 26% for conventional treatment. Hunt & Azrin (1973) found that clients treated in their behavior modification program drank on only 2% of days in a six-month follow-up compared with 55% for traditionally treated patients. These are highly encouraging results which derive from well designed research.

BEHAVIORAL APPROACHES

There are some specific behavioral techniques which should be evaluated with offenders:

BAC Training

Since the early efforts of Lovibond & Caddy (1970), no controlled study has been conducted on the efficacy of training offenders to estimate and control their blood alcohol concentrations by having them ingest alcohol in varying amounts and observing the resultant BAC-levels. There are some obvious problems associated with providing alcohol to offenders which correctional management would wish to resolve, but there may be value in systematically studying the benefits of teaching offenders with alcohol-related problems (through BAC training or video feedback training) the effects of varying amounts of alcohol on their behavior and training them how to behave more adaptively while under the influence of alcohol.

Self-Control Training

Central to Sobell & Sobell's (1973) program was a technique which taught clients to identify cues which appeared to elicit their drinking, and then trained the clients how to avoid those cues or how to respond to them without drinking.

Cue Exposure

An alternative procedure is to extinguish the client's habitual response to these cues by deliberately and systematically overexposing them to them (Hodgson & Rankin, 1976). Flooding or continual exposures without reinforcement (a drink) may extinguish the drinking urge. The success of this technique may be increased if the procedure is supplemented by teaching the client alternative responses to the cues.

Social Skills Training

Many problem-drinkers evidence deficits in social skills. Training in such skills may enable the individual to develop coping behaviors which enable him to deal with interpersonal and other stresses without resorting to alcohol use. The skills include a broad range of vocational, educational and interpersonal behaviors and competencies. Deficits in such skills may give the offender difficulties in job-seeking, relating to employers, marital relationships, and the like. The skills may also include the ability to say "no" when offered "just one more."

Another behavioral technique which might be considered in some correctional settings is teaching appropriate drinking such as drinking slowly rather than gulping drinks and ordering mild or diluted drinks rather than straight liquor. These behaviors can be taught with operant conditioning, i.e. rewarding appropriate drinking behaviors or social behavior while drinking, and punishing inappropriate behaviors (Parades, Gregory & Jones, 1975).

The foregoing techniques can be trained *in vivo* in those situations where drinking is a high probability response (e.g. in bars). They can also be taught in simulated conditions making them adaptable for some correctional settings.

SOBERING THOUGHTS: COGNITIVE PROGRAMS

Most practitioners recognize the necessity of training alcohol-abusing offenders in social skills and in basic life skills, e.g. job-seeking, money management. However, very few correctional alcohol-abuse programs have recognized the necessity of teaching another essential life skill: thinking.

There is a growing body of empirical research which suggests that criminal behavior may be associated with developmental delays in the acquisition of a number of cognitive skills which are essential to social adaptation (Ross & Fabiano, 1982, I & II; 1985).

Research has demonstrated that many offenders have inadequacies in a variety of cognitive functions. For example, they tend to be action-oriented, non-reflective, and impulsive. When faced with a problem or a temptation they immediately respond without stopping to think. They are less likely to *think* about problem situations than to *react* to them. They often "act out" without adequately analyzing the situation, or calculating the consequences of their action. Advice, warnings, or punishment often seem to have little impact on them because they fail to reflect back on their behavior and its effects. Lacking adequate means end reasoning, they respond only to the punishment, not to the message it is intended to convey.

Many offenders have never acquired critical reasoning skills and they evidence a host of thinking errors. The most common of these is externalizing the blame for their actions onto other people or to circumstances "beyond their control." Many fail to consider or appreciate how their behavior and attitudes contribute to the problems they experience.

A number of studies have also demonstrated that many offenders are lacking in interpersonal problem-solving skills. They may evidence deficits in any or all of the following cognitive functions: (a) the ability to recognize the potential for problems when people interact; (b) the ability to consider the consequences of their actions; (c) the ability to generate alternative solutions; (d) the ability to conceptualize the step-by-step means needed to reach their goals; (e) the ability to see the cause and effect relation between their actions and other people's behavior.

Many have not progressed beyond an egocentric stage of cognitive development. They have not learned to distinguish between their own emotional states, thought, and views and those of other people. Lacking the ability to take the pespective of other people, they misread social expectations and misinterpret the actions and intentions of others. Their lack of awareness or sensitivity to other people's thoughts or feelings severely impairs their ability to form acceptable relationships with people (including employers and spouses) and prevents them from developing appropriate means of dealing with inter-personal problems.

Research has demonstrated that such cognitive inadequacies impair the individual's capacity for effective social adjustment and place him at risk for a criminal adjustment. Research has also shown that remediation of these inadequacies is a critical factor in the rehabilitation of juvenile and adult offenders (Ross & Fabiano, 1982). Correctional intervention programs which have included cognitive training techniques have been found to substantially reduce recidivism in both community and institutional settings (Ross & Fabiano, 1985).

The effect of alcohol on higher cognitive functions such as self-criticism, inhibition, impulse control, and judgement is well known (Pernanen, 1978). Alcohol may reduce not only the individual's perceptual abilities but also his ability to abstract, integrate, and communicate. As Pernanen (1976) notes, alcohol may produce,

> "a decrease in the perceived number of behavior cues; a narrowing of the perceptual field. The reduction of cues leads to a more random determination of behavior by the situational (environmental and internal) cues present. Intraindividually, this leads to

> a greater likelihood of affective fluctuations in behavior (and disoriented behavior on the instrumental level) . . . the smaller number of the cues determining behavior . . . leads to a greater likelihood of discrepant structurings of the situation and a consequent cognition of the other's behavior as arbitrary. Perceived arbitrariness of behavior in turn has been shown to lead to aggressive reactions."

One's perceptual and cognitive skills may be severely impaired by excessive use of alcohol and this impairment may place the individual *at risk* in terms of criminal behavior.

Less well recognized is the possibility that for many offenders who abuse alcohol the impairment of their cognitive skills has particularly severe effects on their judgement and behavior because their cognitive skills are not well developed in the first place. The cognitive deficits of such individuals may, in fact, be an important factor in their injudicious, inappropriate and excessive drinking. Moreover, the effect of alcohol on higher cortical functions may severely impair the reasoning of offenders with inadequately developed cognitive skills even when their drinking is less than excessive.

The encouraging results reported for cognitive training programs in correctional treatment suggests that the efficacy of cognitive approaches for alcohol-abusing offenders should be investigated. A wide variety of cognitive training techniques have been developed which may have considerable potential for such offenders (Ross & Fabiano, 1983, Vol 2). They include role-playing and modelling, rational self-analysis, self-control training, means-end reasoning, critical thinking, values education and a variety of cognitive restructuring and cognitive behavior modification techniques.

Offenders may particularly benefit from training in interpersonal cognitive problem-solving which can enhance their ability to recognize and analyze interpersonal problems, lead them to consider the consequences of their behavior, help them to consider alternative courses of action, and help them to understand the thoughts, feelings and behavior of other people (Platt & Duome, 1981).

TRADITIONAL PROGRAMS

Although no traditional programs have been conclusively demonstrated to be effective with offenders with alcohol-related problems, this does not imply that "nothing works." It only means that nothing has been *proven* to "work" in controlled trials. Rather than opting only for innovative programs, resources should be expended on evaluating those more traditional programs which are currently in place.

TREATMENT GOALS

There is now sufficient evidence to support the conclusion that total abstinence need not be the only goal of alcohol treatment (Sobell & Sobell, 1975). Long-term abstinence is rare and many individuals can learn controlled drinking without seriously jeopardizing their social adjustment. For many offenders (at least those who do not have a chronic alcohol problem) controlled drinking may be a more realistic, and a more palatable goal. Many of those offenders whose alcohol-abuse has not been chronic but whose alcohol-related problems have been serious (in personal, social, or legal terms) may be "turned off" by or may "turn away" from programs which require that they give up drinking altogether.

Too many correctional alcohol programs view excessive drinking as a unitary problem rather than as a part of a complex of problems and they treat this problem in a vacuum rather than dealing with it in relation to the other problems which are associated with it. They focus on trying to change drinking attitudes and behaviors and ignore crucial variables (physiological, psychological, social, environmental) which may determine program outcome (Brown & Yalom, 1977). Such problems may be either causes or consequences of problem-drinking, but their treatment may be essential to program success. Our review of the broader correctional literature revealed no effective correctional treatment programs for juvenile and adult offenders which relied on a single therapeutic modality or were directed to a single therapeutic goal. Effective correctional programs are complex — like the offenders they treat.

WHEN TO TREAT?

The results of studies on the relationship between history of drinking and treatment outcome are highly conflicting. However, the old adage that the drinker must "hit bottom" before he can be helped is no longer valid. On the contrary, research now supports the view that it may be essential to intervene early in the drinking career. In fact, waiting till the individual has "hit bottom" may be waiting in vain – research has indicated that the prognosis for skid-row level alcoholics is poor (Fry & Miller, 1976).

LENGTH OF TREATMENT

Although the problem of drop-outs is critical, research on the relationship between outcome and length of stay in treatment has yielded inconsistent results. Some studies with non-offender populations report that longer stay is associated with better outcome, some with no better outcome, and some with poorer outcome (Finney, Moos & Chan, 1981).

Extremely low amounts of treatment may be no more beneficial than no treatment at all (Armor et al., 1978). However, much depends on the characteristics of the client. Some clients undoubtedly improve after very brief treatment contact; however, there is not sufficient evidence to suggest that very short-term treatment should be recommended. It is unlikely that a program can have much impact unless the client attends long enough to obtain a reasonable amount of help.

Nevertheless, remission rates are sometimes high for clients who have only very brief contact with the treatment program. This may reflect the fact that when the individual makes the decision to enter treatment he may be making a decision to change his drinking behavior. For some, making that decision may be all that is required. For these individuals, treatment may contribute relatively little additional impetus to a changed lifestyle. However, for many others, the decision to enter treatment is not sufficient; they require the additional help a program might provide. For these offenders, a longer length of stay may be essential. It is doubtful, however, that very long programs increase the benefits which can accrue from treatment programs of four to eight weeks (Armor et al., 1978). Programs do not need to be either long or lavish. Prolonged and intensive programs appear to be no better than relatively brief programs (Jaffe, 1980).

MOTIVATION

Correctional studies have failed to rule out the possibility that positive results reflect not the potency of treatment but the motivation of the offender. Motivation for treatment *may* be the crucial variable in explaining outcome variance; the best predictor of treatment outcome *may* be the motivation of the offender to seek help rather than the kind of help he obtains. Although this sounds like a truism, it has yet to be convincingly demonstrated in the case of offender populations. Moreover, as we noted earlier, it is likely that for many offenders, motivation is not enough to engender changed drinking behavior. For many offenders, their motivation may be a short-lived response to the adverse consequences of a court-appearance or a jail-term, but with time (often a very short time) they "adapt" and their motivation dissipates. Treatment may be necessary even if only to help sustain the client's motivation.

Treatment may also be required for those whose problematic use of alcohol is associated with a complex number of situational, social, and personal problems which may foster their desire to drink and unless resolved, may destroy their resolve to refrain from drinking. Accordingly, treatment of these problems may be of crucial importance in the maintenance of his motivation to change his drinking behavior.

COMPULSORY TREATMENT

The drop-out rate from alcohol programs is very high. As many as 80% of chronic alcoholics stop treatment before one month; one-third drop out after the initial work-up before treatment even starts (Brandsma et al., 1977). Brandsma et al. (1977) found that only

17% of the clients attended three or more sessions, and that 60% of their clients did not even attend the first session!

In a study of individuals appearing in family court Burke (1977) found that only 1.6% of those with alcohol-abuse problems were willing to accept a treatment referral. She also found that it is not only the alcohol-abuser who rejects alcohol treatment. Their spouses would not seek referral for the alcohol-abuser even though they were the victims and/or the complainants and even when they felt that alcohol abuse was the major cause of the family problems.

Recognizing that no treatment can be effective if the patient does not avail himself of it, many jurisdictions have initiated "compulsory" treatment for offenders with alcohol problems. Typically, this involves giving them a choice between jail and treatment (with or without probation). Similarly, some jurisdictions have (formally or informally) made parole contingent on participation in treatment. There is a considerable debate as to the ethics and legality of enforced treatment and there is also a debate as to whether coercing an offender into treatment has any benefit for him regarding his future social/legal adjustment. Studies by Ball & Weiss (1976), Bjeruer (1972), Bruner-Orne (1951), Chafetz (1965), Laundergan et al. (1979), McGrath et al. (1977), and Pratt (1975) found that coercive treatment was successful, but their evaluations were weak and most included very small samples.

Some studies have found that compulsory programs failed to reduce recidivism (Ditman, Crawford, Forgy, Moskowitz & McAndrew, 1967). However, the success of these programs has not been proven with volunteers and, therefore, their failure with non-volunteers should hardly surprise us! More typically, studies which have compared outcome for court-referred and voluntary patients have found that those coerced into treatment have significantly *poorer* remission rates (Gallant, Bishop, Faulkner, Simpson, Cooper, Lathrop, Brisolara & Bosetta, 1968; Pallone & Tirman, 1978). Coerced patients also drop out of treatment earlier than do self-referred clients (Rubington, 1973; Brandsma et al., 1977).

The negative reports do not establish that coerced clients fail but only that they do not do as well as voluntary clients. This is precisely what one would anticipate given the relationship between intrinsic motivation and positive outcome: the stronger the intrinsic motivation, the better the outcome. Intrinsic motivation may be a better predictor of success than extrinsic motivation; but that remains to be conclusively demonstrated by more adequately designed research. Extrinsic motivation may become intrinsic if the program succeeds in persuading the offender he actually has a problem.

On the other hand, a court-order may be effective in persuading an offender to actually attend the treatment program that, it is hoped, will help him. Nevertheless, drop-out rates are very high even for court-referred clients. Surprisingly, no study seems to have been made as to the likelihood that a drop-out will actually be brought back to court and required to accept the more severe sanction with which he initially was threatened if he failed to attend treatment. It appears that very often there is no adverse consequence to dropping out of enforced treatment. Research is required to determine whether we have coerced only referral and not treatment. Coercion may be more formal than actual.

Additional support for the view that court-enforced treatment in a clinic or social service setting in the community can be more than a technique of deinstitutionalizing the offender with alcohol-related problems is provided by some evidence that coercion can be effective (even essential) in alcohol programs for employees in business settings (e.g. Schramm & Defillippi, 1975). Moreover, an element of coercion is probably involved in the motivation of most individuals who seek treatment. Pressure from relatives, friends, employees, etc., may be less formalized than a court order, but it may be just as potent.

It is regrettable that most studies of the volunteer vs. compulsory treatment issue have measured compulsory treatment only in terms of client outcome and not in terms of cost-benefits and decreases in incarcertion rates.

WHOM TO TREAT?

Correctional alcohol treatment programs have too often been directed to the offender who has been diagnosed as an alcoholic. Many programs systematically reject those whose alcohol problems have not been sufficiently chronic to earn them that label.

This practice has at least two repercussions: (1) It excludes many offenders who, though not alcoholic, may evidence criminal behavior which is strongly related to their use of alcohol. Some offenders use alcohol only intermittently, some not even excessively, but they use it incautiously, indiscriminately, and injudiciously, often with very serious consequences. (2) By labelling program entrants "alcoholics" many offenders are dissuaded from accepting treatment. It is difficult to persuade problem-drinkers to enter treatment if they must accept the "alcoholic" label and what it implies for them: that they are powerless over alcohol and their salvation requires total abstinence . . . forever (Goodrick et al., 1976). Correctional programs should be frequently applied to alcohol *abusers* whose drinking problems may be less chronic, and less severe than those of alcoholics but may have more serious social consequences.

DIFFERENTIAL TREATMENT

Although numerous therapeutic approaches have been used, little comparative research between different treatment modalities has been conducted to determine the relative effectiveness of different approaches for different types of offenders. Offenders are not a homogeneous group. Programs which may be effective for some offenders, may be ineffective for others, and have adverse effects on others. In spite of considerable rhetoric about the need for matching the client to the most suitable treatment, few studies have examined the relationship between correctional alcohol treatment and client characteristics.

There is some evidence which indicates that among offenders, those who are older, more intelligent, better educated, and who have a good employment history and a supportive spouse, and those who have a more accurate perception of the severity of their alcohol problem have a better treatment outcome (Heilbrun, 1971; Pallone & Tirman, 1978). There is also some evidence to suggest that sociopathic traits may be associated with a poor prognosis (Ritson, 1971). The prognosis for chronic skid-row alcoholics has also been found to be poor (Fry & Miller, 1976; Rubington, 1973).

Although it is not yet possible to speak with assurety about which type of treatment works best for which type of offender, research in the general alcohol-treatment literature provides some important suggestions. Thus, Kissin, Platz & Su (1970a & b) found that socially and psychologically intact alcoholics were more likely to accept psychotherapy and reject inpatient rehabilitation, while socially and psychologically unstable alcoholics accepted inpatient rehabilitation. Patients were evaluated not only in terms of degree of abstinence, but also in quality of social and vocational adjustment. Socially intact but psychologically less sophisticated alcoholics were found to do best in drug therapy. Socially and psychologically stable alcoholics had better outcomes in psychotherapy, while socially unstable, but intellectually sophisticated alcoholics did best in inpatient rehabilitation programs. Younger patients did better in inpatient wards. With a heterogeneous alcoholic population it was observed that a greater choice of treatments offered was found to increase over-all success rates (Kissin et al., 1970).

Although there are some methodological problems with this study the results do provide tentative support for differential treatment effectiveness for different client types. In a similar vein, clients who do well on disulfiram (Antabuse) have been found to be older than 42, to have a long history of heavy drinking (16 years), and to be more likely to have had DT's and AA contact, to be abstinent on admission, and to be rated high on motivation by program staff (Baekeland et al., 1971). Depressed patients tend to do poorly on disulfiram (Winship, 1957; Baekeland et al., 1971). Younger patients with rapid progression of alcoholism appear to be poor risks for disulfiram.

TREATMENT MATCHING

These data clearly suggest that no one treatment program will be (maximally) effective for all alcohol abusers. Rather it would appear that in populations which are heterogeneous in composition (particularly with reference to variables such as age, sex, alcohol/drug dependency, intelligence, etc.) a variety of treatment programs will be required. As we noted in our review of the literature on the treatment of the general population of offenders, all effective programs were multi-facetted. They relied not just on one but on a number of treatment modalities to achieve their success.

There are, however, a number of problems associated with a multi-facetted treatment approach. Multi-facetted must not be a euphemism for "smorgasbord" in which any technique is included regardless of its suitability, regardless of whether it is appropriate to the problem, and regardless of its likely contribution to the program's outcome. In the treatment of alcoholism such a "shot gun approach" has been shown by Pattison, Brissindin & Wohl (1967) to be confusing, superfluous and possibly destructive.

Accordingly, it is essential as Skinner (1981) has pointed out, that each of the treatment modalities in a multi-modal program be distinct and powerful and that systematic examination be made of the relative contribution of particular treatment regimens to particular types of clients:

> "Many health care settings offer only one approach . . . to alcoholism, and this package is often multi-modal. Such a treatment regimen makes it nearly impossible to ascertain which components are effective, superfluous, or even deletrious for different types of clients" (Skinner, 1981, p. 363).

Skinner (1981) has presented a "Prototype Model of an Alcoholism Treatment System" which involves differential assignment of clients to treatment. In this model the first step involves the identification of homogeneous subgroups within the alcohol population. These different subgroups are then assigned (following application of a decision rule) to different types of treatment interventions. As a consequence of this differential assignment, it is anticipated that treatment outcomes will be better than would be obtained without treatment matching.

CAN MATCHING WORK?

Although, at first glance, there seem to be conflicting results in the published literature concerning the efficacy of treatment matching, closer scrutiny tends to provide support for matching.

Skinner (1981), in reviewing the empirical evidence, noted that the methodologically superior *experimental* studies (i.e. studies which compare the outcome for clients *randomly* assigned to treatment conditions with clients *matched* to treatments) have consistently supported the matching hypothesis. The kinds of studies which have not provided supportive evidence for matching are methodologically inferior: observational studies, and studies which assess the interactions between client and treatment type using "post hoc" analysis (Moos, Bromet, Tsu & Moos, 1979; Smart, 1978).

For example, McLachlan (1972, 1974) used a quasi-experimental design to assign clients on the basis of their conceptual level to (a) treatment therapists, and (b) after-care therapists. Significantly better outcomes were observed for clients matched to treament or to aftercare therapists than for mismatched clients; 70% vs. 50% improved and 71% vs. 49% improved respectively. Even better results were observed when clients were matched to both treatment and aftercare therapists (matched: 77% improved; mismatched: 38% improved).

In a recent prospective study of patient-treatment matching, McLellan, Woody, Luborsky, O'Brien & Druby (1983) found that when patients treated in their "predicted" program were compared with patients mismatched to treatment, superior six month outcomes for matched patients were observed. Outcomes were on average about 19% better for matched patients.

Of particular interest in this study was the finding that clients who were rated "High Severity" on a global estimate of psychiatric severity at admission had the poorest outcomes, regardless of treatment type. "Low Severity" patients showed the best outcomes regardless of their treatment assignment. Moreover, patients with more severe employment and/or family problems were observed to be less suited to outpatient treatment. The authors, therefore, contend that these severe multi-problem patients should be treated in an extended inpatient rehabilitation program.

The foregoing implies that if we can assume that the offender population is heterogeneous with respect to key prognostic variables, then assessment of clients and assignment to appropriate treatment programs is required in order to maximize the effectiveness of treatment. The next question we must address concerns how we can identify distinct homogeneous subgroups within offender populations.

ASSESSMENT

Clearly, in order to determine the key social/demographic characteristics, personality, perceptual and cognitive attributes for differential treatment of offenders, we need to systematically survey representative samples of relevant offender populations. Because addictions problems seldom, if ever, occur in isolation, the assessment must be multivariate and comprehensive. The assessment must include a specification of:

a) Pertinent social and demographic information; nature and extent of alcohol/drug use; history of use; current pattern of drug use; and degree of dependence.
6) Life-health functioning in the following areas: physical health, emotional health, marital and other social relationships, vocational satisfaction and financial status, leisure-time interests and activities, legal involvement.
c) Client personal resources and potential social support systems.
d) Client treatment preferences.

A number of multivariate assessment instruments and assessment batteries have and are being developed for comprehensive addictions assessment. Examples include the *Addiction Severity Index* (McLellan, Luborsky, O'Brien & Woody, 1980). *A Structured Addictions Assessment Interview for Selecting Treatment* (ASIST) (ARF, 1984), and the *Drinking Behaviour Interview* (Shelton, Hollister & Goche, 1969).

These assessment procedures are, of course, highly dependent on self-report by the offender. Contrary to popular belief, it appears that substance abusers tend to provide accurate information about their consumption patterns and related behaviors when interviewed sober in a clinical setting (Maisto, Sobell & Sobell, 1979; Miller, Crawford & Taylor, 1979). It is generally recommended, however, particularly with correctional clients, that attempts be made to ensure that validity of the assessment by obtaining information by a variety of means and from a variety of sources. These might include, where possible, interviews with significant others, clinical and other official records, and the examination of relevant indices of functioning such as liver tests and intellectual functioning.

Unfortunately, there is very little adequate information available on offender populations with alcohol-related problems which provide sufficient data about personality variables, beliefs, attitudes and life-health functioning in the key areas essential for comprehensive assessment and classification. In the absence of this kind of definitive descriptive information (which would provide the best data base from which to identify homogeneous subgroups, and to then develop treatment programs) we can make some educated guesses about probable subgroup characteristics.

Table 2 presents a summary of the client characteristics which have been suggested to be associated with success in each of 5 different kinds of program services.

Extrapolating from these data and from the known social and demographic characteristics of offender populations, we may tentatively identify four offender subgroups. These are presented in Table 3.

It is important to note that the four groups identified may well overlap. At this state in our knowledge of substance abuse, it is not possible to precisely match clients to treatments. Rather, as Pattison (1982) has noted, treatment matching may currently best be viewed as a general principle which may, given adequate research efforts, result in improved treatment efficacy.

The first group identified is characterized primarily by psychopathology. Given the low success rates reported for these individuals in substance abuse programs (McLellan et al., 1983), offenders who scored high on measures of psychopathology would be generally considered inappropriate (at least initially) for a substance abuse treatment program. Rather, referral to a psychiatric service for appropriate therapy would be considered the most appropriate initial step in treatment planning. Provision of a substance abuse program would be delayed until such time as evidence of diminished psychopathology were found.

The second group identified would be characterized primarily by relatively older age, more years of heavy drinking, and a high degree of alcohol dependence. These offenders would more likely to be successful in a program which had as its philosophical base a "disease model" of alcoholism and one in which the primary rehabilitative goal was abstinence.

Table 2

MATCHING PROGRAM & CLIENT CHARACTERISTICS

	Indications	*Contra-indications*
SELF HELP AA	Male Age > 40 Middle-class Socially Stable Low Psychopathology External LOC High Affiliation Needs Conformist Field – Dependent Cognitive Simplicity	Youth Women
INSTITUTIONAL INPATIENT RESIDENTIAL	Socially & Psychologcially Unstable Intellectually Sophisticated Younger Age > 40	Socially & Psychologically Intact
PHARMACOTHERAPY (e.g. antabuse)	Age > 42 Long Drinking History (> 16 years) History of D.T.'s AA Contact Abstinent on Admission Rated High on Motivation Socially Intact "Less Sophisticated" Psychologically Low Psychopathology	Older
INPATIENT/ RESIDENTIAL	Youth Depressed Rapid Progression of Drinking High Psychopathology	
OUTPATIENT	Social & Psychological Stability	Social & Psychological Instability

The third, and in all likelihood the largest group would be characterized by its (relative) youth, social instability, briefer drinking history, and lower levels of alcohol dependence. Offenders with these characteristics would be more likely to affiliate with a substance abuse program which held as its philosophical base that alcohol abuse is a "learned maladaptive behavior." It is likely that this group would consist of at least two subgroups, differentiated by in-

Table 3

POTENTIAL OFFENDER SUBGROUPS FOR DIFFERENTIAL ALCOHOL ABUSE TREATMENT PLANNING

Primary Characteristics	*Addictions Theory*	*Active Treatment Phase*
A. High Psychopathology	Alcohol Abuse Secondary to Psychopathology	Psychiatric Program
B. Older (> 40), Long Drinking History, High Alcohol Dependence	Disease	Residential Program, Goal: Abstinence AA Model
C. Youth, Single, Socially Unstable, Low Alcohol Dependence i) Intellectually Sophisticated ii) Cognitively Simplistic	Maladaptive Behavior	Extended 6-12 Weeks Rehabilitation Program, Goal: Modified Drinking or Abstinence i) Cognitively Oriented Programs, ii) Behavioral Program: Better for less Educated & Low SES
D. Married and/or Socially Stable	Maladaptive Behavior	Goal: Modified Drinking Brief Interventions, Assessment, and Advice

telligence and conceptual level. The preferred treatment modality would be primarily behavioral in orientation, with a cognitive orientation receiving heavier emphasis in the intellectually more sophisticated group. Behavioral self-control training (Miller, 1978) and individualized behavior therapy (Sobell & Sobell, 1972, 1973; Caddy, Addington & Perkins, 1978) might be particularly appropriate with this subgroup of the offender population.

It is important to note, particularly for this group, that the treatment program would need to incorporate interventions to deal with the other problems identified in assessment; otherwise the efficacy of the alcohol-specific treatment would in all probability be minimized.

The fourth subgroup of offenders would in all likelihood be a small group of relatively socially and psychologically stable individuals for whom alcohol abuse has a short history, and where alcohol dependency is low. Intervention would be minimal, possibly consisting of assessment and individualized advice (Edwards et al., 1976) with extended post release follow-up.

We must emphasize that our suggestions for a classification

model are both speculative and tentative. Very little research has been done to determine the characteristics of different types of offenders who have alcohol-related problems. A national study in the U.S. recently found that there was a negative relationship between heavy drinking and amount of education; the unemployed were more likely to be abstainers and were less likely to be daily drinkers than were the employed; divorced inmates were more likely to be heavy drinkers. However, these data are not sufficient to enable adequate classification for treatment. Empirical research is required in order to validate the existence of relatively homogeneous offender subgroups. Investigation of our proposed classification model might provide a useful first step for such research.

COMBINED ALCOHOL/DRUG PROGRAMS

We might tentatively suggest that a fifth subgroup of offenders may be identified consisting of offenders who have not only an alcohol-abuse problem but also a drug-abuse problem.

Many offenders who have alcohol-related problems also have problems related to the use of other drugs.[16] More than 90% of the alcohol users in a national sample of young men also used other drugs (O'Donnell, Voss, Clayton & Room, 1976). Daily use of alcohol is common among drug users (Preble & Miller, 1977). Weekly poly-drug use is the predominant pattern among individuals entering drug treatment programs and alcohol is a common element in that pattern (Research Triangle Institute, 1980). Since many offenders use both drugs and alcohol dysfunctionally it has been argued that they be treated not in separate settings but together. Combined settings enable more efficient use of personnel, space and financial resources and, therefore, may be more economical. There appears to be little justification for treating the two groups in different settings; in fact, there may be little justification in viewing them as two distinct groups. Poly-drug abuse may be more common than single substance abuse.

Some reports have suggested that the members of each "group" (and their therapists) resent being identified with the other "group" and each group may have strong negative attitudes towards the other, but these problems are not insurmountable in a well-managed environment. A recent study found that alcoholics treated in a conventional setting had a slightly better outcome than those treated in a combined setting (Baker, Lorei, McKnight & Duvall, 1977) but, in general, the evidence about the relative advantages or disadvantages of combined treatment are mixed and inconclusive. Studies on this question have examined the situation in clinic settings. They need to be thoroughly explored in correctional environments. Thus far, there is no strong evidence that would contraindicate combined settings for offender clients.

PROGRAM MANAGEMENT

The majority of correctional programs which reported successful outcomes were conducted within community settings with offenders on probation or in community residential centers or half-way houses. Community programs which were provided exclusively for offender populations were rare. Programs were more likely to be conducted (and funded) by joint arrangements between correctional and social service/health agencies. Given the fact that many individuals in treatment have a criminal history, this would seem to be a reasonable arrangement provided the correctional population is not given short shrift by the agency staff, that the staff has sufficient experience in working with offender populations, and that interagency cooperation is good. Such issues are seldom discussed in the literature. Nor are such questions as whether correctional agency budgets should be spent on developing the agency's own programs and staff or on contracting with other agencies; whether programs should be conducted in long-term institutions or only in short-term ones; at which point in the sentence they should be implemented; or whether the programs should be integrated with the regular institutional services or provided in separate functional units. Such policy-decisions need to be made but the research literature provides few guidelines.

Our review of the broader correctional treatment literature made it clear that effective correctional programs are well-managed programs (Gendreau & Ross, 1979). They ensure that the services which the program purports to provide are actually provided by staff with the requisite skills, industry and persistence. In the correctional alcohol treatment literature, with a few exceptions (Costello et al., 1976, Fry & Miller, 1976), few reports discussed such matters as how they selected and trained their staff, what specific goals the program adopted, how they conceptualized their treatment, or how much treatment their clients actually received. Seldom is mention made of the quality of aftercare supervision.

Alcohol program development must be consistent with systemwide policy and programs must be integrated with established services. As Fry & Miller (1976) have indicated, programs which have goals which conflict with those of the agency or the correctional system and programs whose staff are working at cross-purposes or with little enthusiasm are unlikely to succeed . . . or survive.

PHASES OF ALCOHOL ABUSE TREATMENT

Treatment of alcohol abuse has typically been viewed as a discrete, time-limited event. Recent "systems" formulations of addictions treatment suggest, however, that we need to identify a number of overlapping phases of treatment (Lightfoot, Rosenbaum, Ogurzsoff, Laverty, Kusiar, Barry & Reynolds, 1982; Pattison, 1982). A schematic description of seven phases is presented below. Although these phases are drawn from work in community settings, a similar principle can be applied to treatment programs in correctional institutions.

Table 4

PHASES OF ALCOHOL ABUSE TREATMENT

A	B	C	D	E	F	G
Identification	*Assessment & Referral*	*Entry*	*Active Treatment Phase*	*Monitoring*	*Community Aftercare*	*Follow-up*

Thus far, we have addressed ourselves primarily to the fourth component; the "Active Treatment Phase." This is the phase of treatment which has traditionally received the most attention by practitioners and researchers alike. In recent years, however, a growing body of research evidence has accumulated which suggests that what happens *after* "treatment" may be at least as important, and perhaps more important than what happens *in* "treatment."

It is generally recognized that the environment in which the offender resides after correctional intervention may have a marked effect on his adjustment. The beneficial effects of a program may be diluted or reinforced by the offender's post-treatment experiences. No studies of correctional alcohol programs have examined the relationship between outcome and post-treatment experiences which occur before outcome is measured. The necessity of studying such variables is indicated by recent research which has found that outcome variance among hospital-treated alcoholics was related as much to post-treatment factors as to pre-treatment client characteristics (Finney, Moos & Newborn, 1980; Cronkite & Moos, 1980). "Therapeutic efforts must go beyond the patient to deal with the contexts in which the patient functions after treatment" (Finney et al., 1980, p. 28).

Clients who receive intensive after-care contact following treatment program involvement have been found to have significantly delayed relapse compared to clients not receiving such contact (Ahles, Schulundt, Prue & Rychtarik, 1983). Relapse may be defined as a reinitiation of alcohol or drug use following a period of abstinence, or a return to pre-treatment levels of alcohol or drug use following significant post-treatment decreases in the frequency and or amount of alcohol consumed. It is important to note that relapse is an "expected" part of the rehabilitation process.

> "Any one of a number of stimulus situations may elicit drug consumption even after abstinence has been achieved. For example, environmental stimuli associated either with the positive or negative effects of drugs may act as discriminative stimuli for drug consumption" (Barbarin, 1979, p. 129).

In addition to these conditioning factors, Marlatt and Gordon (1980) have suggested in their analyses of relapse that there are cognitive and affective factors involved in relapse, including attributions regarding effective coping and the abstinence violation effect (AVE).

> "Individuals confronted with situations which challenge their ability to cope may attribute the effective coping entirely to drug use rather than to their own abilities. Thus, individuals may come to feel that drugs provide the only means of coping with difficult situations. Consequently the probability of drug consumption is high when these situations occur. In addition, resumption of drug use after voluntary abstinence leads to cognitive dissonance that may strengthen further drug use. When individuals experience self-controlled abstinence they develop conceptions of themselves as non-drug users. As a result the slightest deviation from total abstinence may lead to dissonance between behaviour and self-attitudes. The perception of self as abstinent, may in the face of contradicting behaviour, lead to guilt, self-blame and a profound sense of failure. To the extent that attributions of failure are internalized they reinforce beliefs about self as hopelessly incurable and provide a rationalization for further violations of abstinence. Thus, if the individual is not prepared for relapse, one minor infraction of abstinence may lead to the belief that all is lost and the process of relapse is completed" (Barbarin, 1979, p. 129).

Any treatment program must prepare participants for relapse. The development of strategies for dealing with urges to drink, provision of reinforcement for alternative adaptive coping behavior and gradual reintroduction into the physical and social "street environment" coupled with ongoing social support will be necessary in order to complete the process of treatment and thus establish a non-substance abusing lifestyle.

Billings and Moos (1983) have recently described three "extra treatment factors" in the recovery-relapse process, including life stressors, coping strategies and social resources. The estimate that post-treatment factors may account for as much as 10-30% of the variance in outcome functioning. After-treatment factors, in effect contribute as much to outcome variance as do treatment factors or the patient's intake symptomatology.

Clearly, for incarcerated populations, where treatment termination may correspond roughly in time with release from incarceration (an extremely stressful readjustment period), the probability of relapse is undoubtedly high. It is during this phase of re-entry that considerable support will be required by the offender as he attempts to stabilize himself in the community setting. Although correctional personnel may monitor released offenders, their role is primarily a "policing" one (not an unnecessary one) which is concerned with the protection of society. With some exceptions, they are unlikely to be perceived by offenders as "therapeutic agent," nor are they likely to be considered a form of "social support." Clearly there is a need for the involvement of third party supervisors, or for the training of correctional personnel so that aftercare supervision can be concerned not only with "social control" but also with "social welfare." These supervisors should possess considerable knowledge about and expertise in the management of alcohol problems. If experience with non-offender populations is applicable, frequent supportive contact over a prolonged period of time following release from correctional facilities may significantly reduce the frequency and severity of relapses in "treated' substance abusing offenders.

CHAPTER 9

EVALUATING CORRECTIONAL ALCOHOL ABUSE PROGRAMS

IT is considered to be unforgivably trite to conclude a book with the hackneyed statement that "more research needs to be done." Nevertheless, that is the most reasonable and the most important conclusion that is warranted in the present case. Most of the research on alcohol treatment in corrections is primitive.

Our review made it clear that because of the failure of correctional agencies to adequately evaluate their programs, only very tentative conclusions can be stated about the current status of alcohol treatment in corrections against which an agency might judge the adequacy of its own current program efforts. Few firm conclusions can be made about which programs have been effective and which have failed. Although we have presented a few recommendations about programs that correctional agencies might implement, these recommendations did not derive from research on correctional alcohol programs but from a much broader literature. The quality of the literature on correctional alcohol treatment jusifies few recommendations.

Research on the effectiveness of correctional treatment for non-alcohol-related offenders and research on the evaluation of alcohol treatment programs in the general population is sufficiently advanced to enable us to provide some guidelines for the evaluation of correctional programs for offenders with alcohol-related problems. The application of these guidelines to current programs should be a priority for correctional agencies which are concerned about offering quality programs for the large number of offenders whose criminal behavior is associated with their use of abuse of alcohol.

The criteria for an adequate evaluation of treatment program effectiveness have been identified in a number of excellent reviews of this issue (Hill & Blane, 1967; Crawford, Chalupsley & Hurley, 1973; Sobell & Sobell, 1980). Generally speaking, Treatment Program Evaluation can most simply be described in terms of the following three phases: I – Treatment Planning, II – Treatment Delivery, and III – Treatment Outcome.

PLANNING

One of the basic requirements of treatment evaluation is that it be planned *prior* to the initiation of the treatment program. *Post hoc,* retrospective evaluations are typically methdologically weak, a factor which seriously limits any conclusions which might be made about program effectiveness. Preplanning allows for identification of appropriate measures, and assignment of clients to groups. It also provides an opportunity to solicit co-operation for follow-up from program participants. Planning involves a specification of who the clients will be (e.g. age, sex), what variables will be measured, and how and when they will be measured. Planning also involves the development of protocols for the treatment program including who will deliver the treatment, when, where, over what period of time, and with what intensity.

Clearly defined behavioral objectives must be developed to enable program evaluators to assess whether treatment has been effective in achieving the goals initially targeted. Often programs have short-term objectives such as increases in problem-solving skills or increased assertiveness, which are assumed to be intervening behaviors (intermediate targets) which must be modified in order for changes in the targeted behaviors (e.g. drinking behavior, employment, or criminal behavior) to be observed. It is essential, therefore, that program planners include procedures for the measurement of these intervening variables if they hope to determine which interventions are effective in changing which targeted behaviors.

In order to test the effectiveness of an assertiveness training program with substance abusers, for example, it would be necesary for program planners to first clearly articulate the relationship between the proposed intervention and alcohol abuse, e.g. increased assertion should lead to decreased alcohol consumption. If the program planners measured only alcohol use prior to and following a treament intervention without assessing changes in assertiveness, they would be unable to ascertain whether the positive or negative outcome of the program in terms of alcohol use was attributable to the assertiveness training aspects of the program. It behooves the evaluator to establish that, (1) assertiveness training was actually provided and that, (2) the training actually improved assertiveness. A particular assertiveness training program which failed to improve assertiveness tells us very little about the value of assertiveness training for alcohol abusers.

Of course, even when measurement of secondary targets is provided, a clear answer to questions about the effects of specific interventions cannot be made without the inclusion of a comparison group, for whom the intervention has not been provided. Ideally clients should be randomly assigned to "treatment" and "control" groups in order to guard against any potential source of bias in group assignment. If random assignment is impossible for pragmatic or other reasons, a quasi-experimental procedure should be employed to provide a reasonable standard against which to assess treatment effects (Campbell & Stanley, 1976).

Client attrition, another potential source of bias in evaluating treatment effectiveness, may also be reduced by careful planning. Agreement from clients to participate in evaluation for an extended post-treatment period of time should be arranged as early as possible in the treatment process. Informed consent for personal contact after treatment is completed, and identification of collateral informants by clients may help to reduce the frequently observed high attrition rates which tend to positively bias outcome conclusions.

TREATMENT DELIVERY

Program implementation must be carefully monitored to ensure that it is delivered in a manner consistent with the original protocol. Thus, program staff should receive comprehensive training in the skills required to deliver the program prior to program implementation. As well, staff performance should be monitored on a periodic basis to ensure that conformity is maintained. Significant departures from the program protocol should be avoided; if changes cannot be avoided, they should be recorded. It is essential that the evaluation determine the degree to which the "treatment" which is *actually* delivered is consistent with that which was developed and described in the planning stage, i.e. with that which was *supposed* to be delivered.

TREATMENT OUTCOME

Because the first six months after treatment is typically an unstable period, longer-term evaluations are recommended. Frequent contact with program participants to monitor and assess the achievement and/or maintenance of therapeutic goals should be conducted for a period up to two years following treatment termination.

When participants do drop out prior to completion of the treatment program, every effort should be made to follow them up in the same way that programs completers are followed. Program evaluations have frequently calculated their outcome statistics using only program completers, a practice which usually leads to erroneously high estimates of program efficacy.

Too many correctional studies have assessed outcome undimensionally and very little information has been gathered about the relationship among the single measures (Maisto & McCallum, 1980). It is becoming increasingly clear in the treatment evaluation literature that measurement must be multi-variate. Alcohol abuse can have wide-ranging effects. Outcome should be measured not only in terms of the client's drinking but also in terms of his emotional, vocational and interpersonal adjustment, his physical health, and his illegal behavior.

Substance abuse problems seldom occur in isolation. Indeed, changes in other areas of life health functioning are usually employed diagnostically in the first place to identify clients with substance abuse problems. Thus, pre-treatment measures should provide a baseline of life-health functioning in a variety of areas. Ideally, these baseline measures should refer to a period of up to one year pre-treatment. It has been agreed that comparing post-treatment drinking with shorter baseline intervals may result in a positively biased estimate of treatment effectiveness, in that a greater number of drunk days is often observed in the one month period preceeding entry into treatment (Maisto & Cooper, 1980).

Participants should be assessed immediately following program completion to determine if short-term objectives have been achieved. Post-treatment arrest records for both alcohol-involved and non alcohol-related offences should be examined. Rather than relying solely on reconviction rates, evaluators should use additional measures which provide information on type and seriousness of offences, frequency of arrests (Sechrest et al., 1979) and temporal intervals between arrests. Whenever possible, evaluators should examine *changes* in criminal behavior by comparing pre-treatment records with post-treatment records (i.e. he should employ both within-subject comparisons and between group comparisons).

It has recently been argued (Sobell & Sobell, 1982) that although self-reports of alcohol abusers are more valid than previously thought, some proportion of self-reports will be invalid. Verification checks on self-reports of drinking behavior can be obtained through such procedures as in-field breath tests or urine tests or tests of liver functioning or through unobtrusive measures of such variables as work attendance (using paycheck stubs) or major life-events (official records of marriage, divorce, etc.). In some instances information on client's drinking can be obtained from collateral sources. The measures chosen to assess program outcome must be valid, reliable and sensitive to change.

Whenever possible, the measures selected should be continuous and quantifiable. Assessing outcome categorically as "abstinent" or "in remission" oversimplifies the nature of alcohol abuse. Much more sensitive measures are required. Temporary relapses are common even among clients who are adjusting well (Polich et al., 1980). Accordingly, assessment should indicate the frequency of relapses or the relative length of time abstinent. Ideally, measurement of drinking behavior should include type and amount of beverage consumed, drinking history, other drug use, time spent drinking, pattern of drinking, and physiological and social consequences of drinking. Such precision may not be easily acquired by correctional researchers, but more refined measures than have been used can and should be employed in assessing program efficacy.

Thus, a variety of sources of outcome data can be used to assess treatment program effectiveness. Because no one of these measures in itself is adequate for assessment, a convergent validity approach using multiple indicators of treatment outcome should be employed from as many sources as possible.

> "When a variety of relatively independent measures of outcome are employed and are mutually corrobative, evaluators can have confidence in the validity of their outcome conclusions" (Sobell & Sobell, 1982, p. 182).

Although treatment evaluation has traditionally been considered difficult if not impossible to conduct, recent developments in the technology of evaluation now make it not only possible but a highly desirable component of any treatment delivery system. Little progress will be made in the treatment of alcohol abusing offenders if program funders do not require systematic evaluation of existing and proposed services.

EXPLANATORY FOOTNOTES

1. The literature search was aided by several computerized bibliographic retrieval services: National Criminal Justice Reference Service; National Institute of Alcohol Abuse and Alcoholism; Criminal Justice Abstracts; Psychological Abstracts; and the National Clearinghouse for Mental Health Information.
2. Shupe's study is one of the few which measured urine alcohol concentrations rather than self-reports or police reports.
3. Many, possibly most, crimes of violence occur in homes and are never reported to the police. The police tend to avoid prosecuting in the case of family disputes. As a result, the strength of the relationship may be underestimated.
4. On the other hand, victims who were drinking at the time of the offence may be more reluctant to report the offence to the police (Pernanen, 1981).
5. The definition of the term "alcoholism" has a lengthy and checkered history. This history has recently been reviewed by Glaser, Greenberg & Barret (1978).
6. Four oz. absolute is approximately equivalent to 9 oz., 40% alcohol.
7. Not an unwelcome move.
8. He also stated in his 1979 apology that "Indeed, it was misleading to judge criminal justice on the basis of these evaluation studies." This, it should be mentioned, appeared in a footnote.
9. Gottfredson (1980) suggests that most correctional treatment programs have not been based on a medical model; they have been based on no model at all!

10. The term "intervention" may be better, but it is too all-encompassing.
11. Older inmates were more likely to receive treatment than younger ones. (Petersilia, 1979).
12. LSD was thought to facilitate cathartic experiences and insight.
13. The use of drugs in treatment does *not* necessarily imply the acceptance of the view that alcoholism is an illness or a disease which has an origin in biological malfunction.
14. Psychodynamic therapies are usually based on a model of alcoholism as a symptom of underlying psychopathology. The popularity and acceptability of this view continues to wane.
15. Some educational programs for substance abusers in corrections are very sophisticated. For example, Schmidt, Burchief & Myers (1977) have described a program which has offered for drug-abusers at San Quentin which consisted of a university undergraduate course in psychopharmacology!
16. As Collins (1980) points out, we do not yet fully understand psychopharmacological effects of multi-drug use. The effects may be dramatic. For example, the simultaneous use of alcohol and barbiturates produces an additive effect from the ingestion of even small amounts of both together as the effect of one potentiates the effect of the other and vice versa.

REFERENCES

Adams, S.: A way out of the rhetoric. In *Rehabilitation, Recidivism and Research.* Hackensack, National Council on Crime and Delinquency, 1976.

Adams, S.: Evaluating correctional treatments: toward a new perspective. *Criminal Justice and Behavior, 4,* 323-329, 1977.

Ahles, T., Schlundt, D.A., Prue, D., and Rychtarik, R.: Impact of aftercare arrangements on maintenance of treatment success in abusive drinkers. *Addictive Behaviors, 8,* 53-58, 1983.

Alexander, J.F., Barton, C., Schiaro, R.S., and Parsons, B.V.: Systems-behavioral intervention with families of delinquents: therapist characteristics and family behavior outcome. *Journal of Consulting & Clinical Psychology, 44,* 656-664, 1976.

Alexander, J.F. and Parsons, R.J.: Short-term behavioral intervention with delinquent families: impact on family process and recidivism. *Journal of Abnormal Psychology, 81,* 219-225, 1973.

Amir, M.: *Patterns of Forcible Rape.* Chicago, University of Chicago Press, 1971.

Anant, S.S.: Former alcoholics and social drinking: an unexpected finding. *The Canadian Psychologist, 9,* 35, 1968.

Andrews, D.A. and Kiessling, J.J.: Program structure and effective correctional practices. In Ross, R.R. and Gendreau, P. (Eds.): *Effective Correctional Treatment.* Toronto, Butterworths, 1980.

Annis, M.: Group treatmentof incarcerated offenders with alcohol and drug problems: a controlled evaluation. *Canadian Journal of Criminology, 21,* 3-15, 1979.

Annis, N.M. and Chan, D.: Differential treatment assignment: empirical evidence from a typology of adult offenders. *Criminal Justice and Behavior, 10,* 159-173, 1983.

Annis, H. and Smart, R.G.: Arrests, readmissions and treatment following release from detoxication centres. *Journal of Studies on Alcohol, 39,* 1276-1283, 1978.

A.R.F.: *Structured Addiction Assessment Interview for Selecting Treatment* (A.S.I.S.T).

Toronto, Alcoholism and Drug Addiction Research Foundation, 1984.

Armor, D.: The Rand Reports: Reconciling Research and Treatment Perspectives. In Evaluation of the Alcoholic: Implications for Research, Theory, and Treatment. NIAAA Research Monograph-5 Rockville, Maryland, 1981.

Armor, D.J., Polich, J.M., and Stambul, H.B.: *Alcoholism and Treatment: A Rand Corporation Research Study.* New York, Wiley, 1978.

Arnold, J.E., Levine, A.G., and Patterson, G.R.: Changes in sibling behavior following family intervention. *Journal of Consulting and Clinical Psychology, 5,* 683-688, 1975.

Azrin, N.H.: Improvements in the community — reinforcement approach to alcoholism. *Behavior Research and Therapy, 339-348,* November, 1976.

Bach-y-Rita, G., Lion, J.R., and Ervin, F.R.: Pathological intoxication: clinical and electroencephalographic studies. *American Journal of Psychiatry, 127,* 698-703, 1970.

Baekeland, F., Lundwall, L., and Kissen, B.: Method for the treatment of chronic alcoholism: a critical appraisal. In Gibbins, R.J. (Ed.): *Research Advances in Alcohol and Drug Problems.* Toronto, Wiley, 1975.

Bailey, H.B. and Stewart, J.: Normal drinking by former problem drinkers. *Quarterly Journal of Studies on Alcohol, 28,* 308-315, 1967.

Bailey, W.C.: Correctional outcome: an evaluation of 100 reports. *Journal of Criminology and Police Science, 57,* 153-160, 1966.

Bakan, D.: *Slaughter of the Innocents: a Study of the Battered Child Phenomenon.* Boston, Beacon Press, 1971.

Baker, S.L., Lorei, T., and McNight, H.A.: The veterans administration's comparison study: alcoholism and drug abuse — combined and conventional treatment settings. *Alcoholism: Clinical and Experimental Research, 1,* 285-291, 1977.

Bales, R.F.: Cultural differences in rates of alcoholism. *Quarterly Journal of Studies on Alcohol, 6,* 480-499, 1946.

Ball, M.: Issues of violence in family casework. *Social Casework,* 3-12, January, 1977.

Ball, J.H. and Weiss, C.W.; Police officers as community organizers. *Police Chief, 18,* 46-47, 1976.

Bannay, R.S.: Alcoholism and crime. *Quarterly Journal of Studies on Alcohol, 2,* 686-716, 1942.

Barbarin, D.: Recidivism in drug addiction: a behavioral analysis. *Addictive Behaviors, 4,* 121-132, 1979.

Belasco, J.A.: The criterion question revisited. *British Journal of Addiction, 66,* 39-44, 1971.

Benor, D. and Ditman, K.S.: Tranquilizers in the management of alcoholics. A review of literature to 1964, Part II. *Journal of Criminal Pharmacology, 7,* 17-25, 1967.

Berlinger, A.K.: *Developing a treatment program for the alcoholic offender in confinement.* Paper presented at Texas Commission on Alcoholism's 16th Annual Institute of Alcohol Studies, Austin, Texas, July 23, 1973.

Billings, A.G. and Moos, R.N.: Psychosocial processes of recovery among alcoholics and their families: implications for clinicians and program evaluators. *Addictive Behaviors, 8,* 205-218, 1983.

Bjeruer, K.B.: Punishment or treatment for intoxicated drivers. *Blutalkohol, 9,* 59-62, 1972.

Blakely, C.H., Davidson, W.S., Saylor, C.A., and Robinson, M.J.: Kentfields rehabilitation program: ten years later. In Ross, R.R. and Gendreau, P. (Eds.): *Effective Correctional Treatment.* Toronto, Butterworths, 1980.

Blumstein, A., Cohen, J., and Nagin, D. (Eds.): *Deterrence and Incapacitation: Estimating the Effects of Criminal Sanctions on Crime Rates.* Washington, D.C., National Academy of Sciences, 1978.

Boland, E. and Wilson, J.Q.: Age, crime and punishment. *The Public Interest, 51,* 22-34, 1978.

Boland, F.J., Mellor, C.S., and Revusky, S.: Chemical aversion treatment of alcoholism: lithium as the aversion agent. *Behavior Research and Therapy, 16,* 401-409, 1978.

Brandsma, J.M. and Maultsby, M.C.: The court-probated alcoholic and outpatient treatment attrition. *British Journal of Addiction, 72,* 23-30, 1977.

Brandsma, J.M., Maultsby, M.C., and Welsh, R.J.: *The Outpatient Treatment of Alcoholism: A Review and Comparative Study.* Baltimore, University Park Press, 1980.

Bromet, E. and Moos, R.H.: Environmental resources and the post-treatment functioning of alcoholic patients. *Journal of Health and Social Behavior, 18,* 326-338, 1977.

Brown, S. and Yalom, K.: Interactional group therapy with alcoholics. *Journal of Studies of Alcohol, 38,* 426-456, 1977.

Bruner-Orne, M.: A court-clinic for alcoholics. *Quarterly Journal of Studies on Alcohol, 12,* 592-600, 1951.

Burke, S.: *Alcohol Use and its Relationship to Involvement with the Provincial Court (Family Division), Judicial District of York (Etobicoke).* Islington, Ontario, The Etobicoke Family Court Committee, 1977.

Byles, J.A.: Violence, alcohol programs and other problems in disintegrating families. *Journal of Studies on Alcohol, 39,* 551-553, 1978.

Caddy, G.: A review of problems in conducting alcohol treatment outcome studies. In Sobell, L., Sobell, M. and Ward, E. (Eds.): *Evaluating Alcohol and Drug Abuse Treatment Effectiveness Recent Advances.* New York, Pergammon, 1980.

Caddy, G.R. and Addington, H.J., and Perkins, J.: Individualized behavior therapy for alcoholics: a third year independent double-blind follow-up. *Behavior Research and Therapy, 16,* 345-362, 1978.

Cadogan, D.A.: Marital group therapy in the treatment of alcoholism. *Quarterly Journal of Studies on Alcohol, 34,* 1187-1194, 1973.

Cahalan, D.: *Problem Drinkers, a National Survey.* San Francisco, Jossey-Bass, 1970.

Cahill, J.: *Stafford County Multi-County Drug and Alcohol Treatment Program.* Concord, New Hampshire Governor's Commission on Crime and Delinquency, 1979.

Campbell, D.T. and Stanley, J.C.: *Experimental and Quasi-Experimental Designs for*

Research. Chicago, Rand McNally, 1966.

Carpenter, J.A. and Armenti, N.P.: Some effects of ethanol of human sexual and aggressive behavior. In Kissin, D. (Ed.): *The Biology of Alcoholism.* New York, Plenum Press, 1972.

Chafetz, M.E.: Is compulsory treatment of the alcoholic effective? *Northwest Medicine, 65,* 932-937, 1965.

Chandler, M.J.: Egocentrism and antisocial behavior: the assessment and training of social perspective – taking skills. In Ross, R.R. and Gendreau, P. (Eds.): *Effective Correctional Treatment.* Toronto: Butterworths, 1980.

Chaneles, S.: A look at Martinson's report. *Fortune Society News, 3,* 12-16, 1975.

Chaneles, S.: Prisoners can be rehabilitated now. *Psychology Today, 10,* 129-133, 1976.

Clare, A.W.: How good is treatment? In Edwards, G. and Grant, M. (Eds.): *Alcoholism: New Knowledge and New Responses.* London, Croon Helm, 1977.

Clay, T.R. & Swenson, P.R.: *Effectiveness of the Pheonix ASAP's DWT School and Alcohol Awareness Program in Reducing DWI Arrest Recidivism.* Manuscript submitted for publication.

Coffler, D.B. and Hadley, R.G.: The residential rehabilitation centre as an alternative to jail for chronic drunkenness offenders. *Quarterly Journal of Studies on Alcohol, 34*(4), 1180-1186, 1973.

Cohen, M., Liebson, J.A., Faillace, L.A., and Speers, W.: Alcoholism: controlled drinking and incentives for abstinence. *Psychological Reports, 28,* 575-580, 1971.

Coleman, D.H. and Straus, M.A.: *Alcohol Abuse and Family Violence.* Paper presented at the Annual Meeting f the American Sociological Association. Boston, August 1979.

Collier, D. and Somfay, S.A.: Ascent from skid row. *Addictions, 21*(3), 28-47, 1974.

Collins, J.J.: Alcohol use and criminal behavior: an empirical, theoretical and methodological review. In Collins, J.J. (Ed.): *Drinking and Crime: Perspectives on the Relationships between Alcohol Consumption and Criminal Behavior.* New York, The Guilford Press, 1981.

Collins, J.J.: *Drinking and Crime: Perspectives on the Relationships between Alcohol Consumption and Criminal Behavior.* New York, The Guilford Press, 1981.

Cook, S.A.: Criminal behavior and the use of beverage alcohol. *Canadian Journal of Corrections, 4,* 83-102, 1962.

Corder, B.F., Corder, B.F., and Laidlaw, N.D.: An intensive treatment program for alcoholics and their wives. *Quarterly Journal of Studies on Alcohol, 33,* 1144-1146, 1972.

Correctional Services, Canada, Offenders Programs. *Survey of Programs,* 1981.

Costello, R.M., Giffen, M.B., Schneider, S.L., Edginton, P.W., and Manders, K.R.: Comprehensive alcohol treatment planning, implementation, and evaluation. *International Journal of Addictions, 11,* 553-570, 1976.

Costello, R.M., Bechtel, J.E., and Giffen, M.B.: A community's efforts to attack the problem of alcoholism. *International Journal of Addiction, 8*(6), 875-888,

1973.

Costello, R.M.: Alcoholism treatment programming: historical trends. In Madden, J.S., Walker, R. and Kenyon, W.H. (Eds.): *Alcoholism and Drug Dependence: A Multidisciplinary Approach.* New York, Plenum Press, 1977.

Cox, S.G.: Rational behavior training as a rehabilitative program for alcoholic offenders. *Offender Rehabilitation, 3*(3), 245-256, 1979.

Crawford, J.J., Chalupsley, A.B., and Hurley, M.H.: *The Evaluation of Psychological Approaches to Alcoholism Treatments: A Methodological Review.* American Institute for Research Final Report, AIR-96502-3/73-FR, Palo Alto, California, 1973.

Cronkite, R.C. and Moos, R.H.: Determinants of the post-treatment functioning of alcoholic patients: a conceptual framework. *Journal of Consulting and Clinical Psychology, 48,* 305-316, 1980.

Cuthbert, T.M.: A portfolio of murders. *British Journal of Psychiatry, 116,* 1-10, 1970.

Davies, D.L.: Normal drinking in recovered alcoholics. *Quarterly Journal of Studies on Alcohol, 23,* 94-104, 1962.

Department of Justice: Prisoners and alcohol. *Bureau of Justice Statistics Bulletin.* Washington, D.C., U.S. Department of Justice, 1983.

Ditman, K.S., Crawford, G.G., Forgy, E.W., Moskowitz, H., and Macandrew, G.: A controlled experiment on the use of court probation for drunk arrests. *American Journal of Psychiatry, 124*(2), 160-163, 1967.

Duncan, J.W. and Duncan, G.M.: Murder in the family: a study of homicidal adolescents. *American Journal of Psychiatry, 127,* 1498-1502, 1971.

Edwards, G. and Grant, M.: *Alcoholism Treatment in Transition.* Baltimore: University Park Press, 1980.

Edwards, G., Gross, M.M., Keller, J., Moser, J., and Room, R.: *Alcohol-Related Disabilities.* Offset Publication Number 32. World Health Organization, Geneva, 1977.

Edwards, G., Orford, J., Egert, S., Guthrie, S., Hawkin, A., Hinsman, C., Milchelson, M., Oppenheimer, E, and Taylor, C.: Alcoholism: a controlled trial of treatment and "advice". *Journal of Studies on Alcohol, 38,* 1004-1031, 1977.

Elli, F.: *The Riot.* New York, Avon, 1966.

Emrick, C.D.: A review of the psychologically-oriented treatment of alcoholism: the relative effectiveness of different treatment approaches and the effectiveness of treatment vs. no treatment. *Journal of Studies on Alcohol, 36,* 88-108, 1975.

Emrick, C.D.: A review of psychologically-oriented treatment of alcoholism: the use and interrelationships of outcome criteria and drinking behavior following treatment. *Quarterly Journal of Studies on Alcohol, 35,* 523-549, 1974.

Engle, K.B. and Williams, T.K.: Effect of an ounce of vodka on alcoholics' desire for alcohol. *Quarterly Journal of Studies on Alcohol, 33,* 1099-1105, 1972.

Epstein, J.S. and Taylor S.P.: Instigation to aggression as a function of degree of defeat and perceived aggresive intent of the opponent. *Journal of Personality, 35,* 265-289, 1967.

Erskine, H.: Alcohol and the criminal justice system: challenge and response. Washington, National Institute of Law Enforcement and Criminal Justice, January, 1972.

Esser, P.H.: Conjoint family therapy with alcoholics — a new approach. *British Journal of the Addictions, 64,* 275-286, 1970.

Evard, F.H.: *Alcohol and the Parolee, in Successful Parole.* Springfield, Charles C Thomas, 1971.

Eyeberg, S. and Johnson, S.M.: Multiple assessment of behavior modification with families: effects of contingency contracting and order of treated persons. *Journal of Consulting and Clinical Psychology, 42,* 594-604, 1974.

Fattach, E.A.: A critique of deterrence research with particular reference to the economic approach. *Canadian Journal of Criminology, 24,* 79-90, 1982.

Finney, J.W. and Moos, R.H: Treatment and outcome for empirical subtypes of alcoholic patients. *Journal of Consulting and Clinical Psychology, 47*(1), 25-38, 1975.

Finney, J.W., Moos, R.H., and Newborn, C.R.: Post-treatment experiences and treatment outcome of alcoholic patients six months and two yers after hospitalization. *Journal of Consulting and Clinical Psychology, 48,* 17-29, 1980.

Finney, J.W., Moos, R.H., and Chan, D.A.: Length of stay and program component effects in the treatment of alcoholism: a comparison of two techniques for process analysis. *Journal of Consulting and Clinical Psychology, 49,* 120-131, 1981.

Fishman, R.: *Criminal Recidivism in New York City.* New York, Praeger Publishers, 1977.

Flynn, J.P.: Recent findings related to wife abuse. *Social Casework,* 13-20, January, 1977.

Fogel, D.: *We Are The Living Proof: The Justice Model for Corrections.* Cincinatti, Anderson, 1975.

Fox, R.: A multidisciplinary approach to the treatment of alcoholism. *American Journal of Psychiatry, 723,* 769-778, 1967.

Frank, C.H., Mooney, W.C., and Payloff, G.C.: *Proceedings of the Seminar on Alcoholism Detection Treatment and Rehabilitation within the Criminal Justice System.* Washington, D.C., L.E.A.A., 1973.

French, O.: *The Globe & Mail.* Toronto, March 3, 1984.

Fry, L.J. and Miller, J.: Responding to skid row alcoholism: self-defeating arrangements in an innovative treatment program. *Social Problems,* 665-688, 1976.

Gallant, D.M., Bishop, M.P., Faulkner, M.A., Simpson, L., Copper, A., Lathrop, D., Brisolara, A.M., and Bosetta, J.R.: A comparative evaluation of compulsory treatment of the chronic alcoholic municipal court offender. *Psychosomatics, 9*(6), 306-310, 1968.

Gay, M.: Pretrial release and diversion for alcoholism treatment and rehabilitation. *NIAAA,* 1973.

Gelles, R.J.: Child abuse as psychopathology: a sociological critique and reformulation. *American Journal of Orthopsychiatry, 43,* 611-621, 1973.

Gelles, R.J.: *The Violent Home.* Beverly Hills, Sage, 1974.

Gendreau, P. and Ross, R.R.: Effective correctional treatment: bibliotherapy for cynics. *Crime and Delinquency, 25,* 463-489, 1979.

Gendreau, P. and Ross, R.R.: Correctional potency: treatment and deterrence on trial. In Roesch, R. and Corrado, R.R.: *Evaluation and Criminal Justice Policy.* Beverly Hills, Sage, 1981.

Gerard, D.L. and Saenger, G.: *Outpatient Treatment of Alcoholism. A Study of Outcome and its Determinants.* Toronto, University of Toronto Press, 1966.

Getlow, S.E.: Alcoholism, a disease. In Bourne, P.E. and Fox, R. (Eds.): *Alcoholism: Progress in Research and Treatment.* New York, Academic Press, 1973.

Gil, D.G.: Violence against children. *Journal of Marriage and the Family, 33,* 637-648, 1971.

Gibbs, J.P.: Law as a means of social control. In Gibbs, J.P. (Ed.): *Social Control: Views from the Social Sciences.* Beverly Hills, Sage Press, 1982.

Glaser, F.B., Breenberg, S.W., and Barret, M.: *A Systems Approach to Alcohol Treatment.* Toronto, Alcohol Research Foundation, 1978.

Glaser, D. and O'Leary, V.: *The Alcoholic Offender.* Washington, D.C., National Parole Institute, 1973.

Goldstein, G.: The significance of perception and cognition in understanding the alcoholic. In Goldstein, G. and Neuringer, C. (Eds.): *Empirical Studies of Alcoholism.* Cambridge, Ballinger, 1976.

Goodman, L.S. and Gilman, A.: In Mayer, S. and Melman, K.L. (Eds.): *The Pharamacological Basis of Therapeutics,* 6th edition. New York, Macmillan, 1980.

Goodrick, D.D., Vigdal, G., and Sutton, D.: Emerging directions in alcohol treatment: new hope for the problem-drinking offender. *Offender Rehabilitation, 1*(1), 57-66, 1976.

Goodwin, D.W., Crane, J.B., and Guse, S.B.: Felons who drink: an 8-year follow-up. *Quarterly Journal of Studies on Alcohol, 32,* 136-147, 1971.

Goodwin, D.W.: Alcohol in suicide and homicide. *Quarterly Journal of Studies on Alcohol, 14*(1), 151-159, 1973.

Gottfredson, M.R.: Treatment destruction techniques. In Ross, R.R. and Gendreau, P.: *Effective Correctional Treatment.* Toronto, Butterworths, 1980.

Gove, W.: Sleep deprivation. *American Journal of Psychiatry, 124,* 133-142, 1967.

Gove, W.R.: Sleep deprivation: a cause of psychotic disorganization. *American Journal of Sociology, 75,* 782-799, 1969.

Greenberg, S.W.: Alcohol and crime: a methodological critique of the literature. In Collins, J.J.: *Drinking and Crime: Perspectives on the Relationships between Alcohol Consumption ad Criminal Behaviors.* New York, Guilford, 1981.

Greenberg, D.F.: The correctional effects of corrections: a survey of evaluations. In Greenberg, D.F. (Ed.): *Corrections and Punishments.* Beverly Hills, Sage, 1977.

Griswold, H..: *An Eye for an Eye.* New York, Holt, Rinehart & Winston, 1970.

Grossman, J.E. and MacDonald, D.G.: Alcohol abuse research. *Corrections Today,* 20, October, 1983.

Guze, S.B. and Cantwell, D.P.: Alcoholism, parole observations and criminal recidivism: a study of 116 parolees. *American Journal of Psychiatry, 122,* 436-439, 1965.

Guze, S.B., Goodwin, D.W., and Crane, J.B.: Criminality and psychiatric disorders. *Archives of General Psychiatry, 20,* 583-591, 1969.

Guze, S.B., Tuason, V.B., Gatfield, P.D., Stewart, M.A., and Picken, B.: Psychiatric illness and crime with particular reference to alcoholism: a study of 223 criminals. *Journal of Nervous and Mental Disease, 134*(6), 512, 1962.

Hagan, J.: *Deterrence Reconsidered: Methodological Innovations.* Beverly Hills, Sage, 1982.

Haines, D.: Alcoholism in prisons. *International Journal of Offender Therapy, 22*(2), 127-132, 1978.

Hall, R.W.: Alternative to the criminality of driving while intoxicated. *Journal of Police Science and Administration, 5*(2), 138-144, 1977.

Halleck, S.L. & Witte, A.D.: Is rehabilitation dead? *Crime and Deliquency, 23,* 372-381, 1977.

Hamilton, C.J. and Collins, J.J.: The role of alcohol in wife beating and child abuse: a review of the literature. In Collins, J.J.: *Drinking and Crime: Perspectives on the Relationships between Alcohol Consumption and Criminal Behavior.* New York: Guilford, 1981.

Hamilton, J.R.: Evaluation of a detoxification service for habitual drunken offenders. *British Journal of Psychiatry, 135,* 28-34, 1979.

Hayman, M.: Current attitudes to alcoholism of psychiatrists in Southern California. *American Journal of Psychiatry, 112,* 484-493, 1956.

Hayslip, B., Kapusiaski, D., Darbes, A., and Zer, R.: Evaluations of driving while intoxicated programs: some methodological considerations. *Journal of Studies on Alcohol, 37,* 1742-1746, 1976.

Heath, D.B.: A critical review of ethnographic studies of alcohol use. In Gibben, R., Israel, Y., Kalant, H., Popham, R.E., Schmidt, W., and Smart, R.G.: *Research Advances in Alcohol andDrug Problems,* Vol. 2. New York, Wiley, 1975.

Hedberg, A. G. and Campbell, R.: A comparison of four behavioral treatments of alcoholism. *Journal of Behaviour Therapy and Experimental Psychiatry, 5,* 251-256, 1974.

Heilbrun, A.: Prediction of rehabilitation outcome in chronic out-care alcoholics. *Quarterly Journal of Studies on Alcohol, 32*(2), 328-333, 1971.

Herman, V., Sesko, M., Trinajstic, M., Vidovic, V., and Cabrijan, T.: Hypoglycemic conditions in the course of chronic alcoholism. *Alcoholism, 6,* 87-90, 1970.

Hill, M.I. and Blane, H.T.: Evaluation of psychotherapy with alcoholics: a critical review. *Quartely Journal of Studies of Alcohol, 28,* 76-104, 1967.

Hodgson, R. and Rankin, H.: Modification of excessive drinking by cue exposure. *Behavior Research and Therapy, 14,* 305-307, 1976.

Hoffs, E.C.: The use of pharmacological adjuncts in the psychotherapy of alcoholics. *Quarterly Journal of Studies on Alcohol,* Supplement #1, 138-150, 1961.

Holden, R.T.: Rehabilitative sanctions for drunk driving: an experimental evaluation. *Journal of Research in Crime and Delinquency, 20*(1), 55-72, 1983.

Hunt, C.M. and Azrin, N.H.: A community-reinforcement approach to alcoholism. *Behavior Research and Therapy,* 91-104, February, 1973.

Institute for Scientific Analysis: *Drinking Patterns and Criminal Careers. A Study of 310 Imprisoned Male Felons.* San Francisco, Scientific Analysis Corporation, 1978.

Jaffe, J.H.: What alcoholism isn't borrowing. In Edwards, G. and Grant, M.: *Alcoholism Treatment in Transition.* Baltimore, University Park Press, 1980.

Jeffrey, R. and Woolpert, S.: Work furlough as an alternative to incarceration: an assessment of its effects on recidivism and social cost. *Journal of Criminal Law and Criminology, 65,* 405-415, 1974.

Jellinek, E.M.: *The Disease Concept and Alcoholism.* New Haven, Millhouse Press, 1960.

Jesness, C.: Comparitive effectiveness of behavior modification and transanctional analysis programs for delinquents. *Jouranl of Consulting and Clinical Psychology, 43*(6), 658-779, 1975.

Johnson, L.C., Burdick, J.A. & Smith, J.: Sleep during alcohol intake and withdrawal in the chronic alcoholic. *Archives of General Psychiatry, 22,* 406-418, 1970.

Johnson, J.F.: The results of family therapy with juvenile offenders. *Juvenile Justice,* 29-33, November, 1977.

Johnson, S.D., Gibson, L., and Linden, R.: Alcohol and rape in Winnipeg, 1966-1975, *Journal of Studies on Alcohol, 39*(11), 1877-1894, 1978.

Jones, R.K.: Alcohol and highway crashes: a projection for the 1980s. *University of Michigan Highway Safety Research Institute Reseach Review, 7,* 1-16, 1977.

Julian, A. and Kilmann, P.R.: Group treament of juvenile delinquents: a review of the outcome literature. *International Journal of Group Psychotherapy, 29*(1), 3-37, 1979.

Kalant, N., LeBlanc, A.E., and Gibbins, R.J.: Tolerance to and dependence on, some non-opiate psychotropic drugs. *Pharmacological Review, 23,* 185-191, 1971.

Kalb, M.: The myth of alcoholism prevention. *Preventive Medicine, 4,* 404-416, 1975.

Kalish, C.B.: Prisoners and alcohol. *Bureau of Justice Statistics Bulletin,* January, 1983.

Kassebaum, G., Ward, D. and Wilner, D.: *Prison Treatment and Parole Survival: An Empirical Assessment.* New York, Wiley, 1971.

Kendell, R.E.: Normal drinking by former alcohol addicts. *Quarterly Journal of Studies on Alcohol, 26,* 247-257, 1965.

Kennedy, D.J.: The Rideau alcohol program. A multidisciplinary approach to alcohol-related problems of incarcerated offenders. *Canadian Journal of Criminology, 22,* 428-442, 1980.

Kent, R.N. and O'Leary, K.D.: A controlled evaluation of behavior modification with conduct problem children. *Journal of Consulting and Clinical Psychology, 144,* 586-596, 1976.

Kissin, B., Platz, A., and Su, W.H.: Social and psychological factors in the treatment of chronic alcoholism. *Journal of Psychiatric Research, 8,* 13-27, 1970(a).

Kissin, B., Platz, A., Su, W.H.: Selective factors in treatment choice and outcome in alcoholics. In Mello, N.K. and Mendelson, J.H. (Eds.): *Recent Advances in Studies on Alcoholism.* Washington, D.C., U.S. Government Printing Office, 1970(b).

Kissin, B.: Comments on alcoholism: a controlled trial of "treatment" and "advice". *Journal of Studies on Alcohol, 38,* 1804-1808, 1977.

Kinder, B.N., Pope, N.E. and Walfish, S.: Drug and alcohol education programs: a review of outcome studies. *International Journal of Addictions, 18*(7), 1035-1052, 1980.

Klockars, C.B.: The true limits of the effectiveness of correctional treatment. *The Prison Journal, 55,* 53-64, 1975.

Knott, D.N. and Beard, J.D.: *The Disease Concept of Alcoholism.* Paper presented at the 115th (1966) Annual Meeting of the American Medical Association, 1966.

Knupfer, G. and Room, R.: Age, sex and social class as factors in a metropolitan community. *Social Problems, 12,* 224-240, 1964.

Lambert, L.R. and Madden, P.G.: *Adult Female Offenders before-during-after Incarceration. Summary Conclusions and Recommendations.* Ontario, Ministry of Correctional Services, 1975.

Landstreet, B.F.: *Drinking Driver — The Alcohol Safety Action Program.* Springfield, Charles C Thomas, 1977.

Lang, A.R., Goeckner, D.J., Adesso, V.J., and Marlatt, G.A.: Effects of alcohol on aggression in male social drinkers. *Journal of Abnormal Psychology, 84*(5), 508-518, 1975.

Laundergan, J.C., Spicer, J.W., and Kammeier, M.L.: *Are Court Referrals Effective? Judicial Commitment for Chemical Dependency in Washington Coutny, Minnesota.* Minneapolis, Hazelden Research Foundation, 1979.

Lee, R. and Haynes, N. McG.: Project CREST and the dual-treatment approach to delinquency: methods and research summarized. In Ross, R.R. and Gendreau, P. (Eds.): *Effective Correctional Treatment.* Toronto, Butterworths, 1980.

Lenke, L.: Valdbrott och alkohol: *En studie i misshandelsbrottslighetens utveckling* (Violent crime and alcohol: a study of the developments in assaultive crime). Stockholm, Department of Criminology, University of Stockholm, 1975.

Lewis, C.S.: The humanitarian theory of punishment. In Grupp, S.E. (Ed.): *Theories of Punishment.* Bloomington, Indiana University Press, 304-307, 1970.

Levinson, T. and Sereny, G.: An experimental evaluation of insight therapy for the chronic alcoholic. *Can. Psychiatr. Assoc. J., 14,* 143-146, 1969.

Lightfoot, L.O., Rosenbaum, P., Ogurzsoff, S., Laverty, G., Kusiar, S., Barry, K., and Reynolds, W.: *Final Report of the Kingston Treatment Programme Development Research Project.* Kingston, Queen's University, 1982.

Lindelius, R. and Salum, J.: Alcoholism and criminality. *Acta Psychiatrica Scandinavia, 49,* 306-314, 1973.

Lloyd, R.W. and Salzberg, H.C.: Controlled social drinking: an alternative to abstinence as a treatment goal for alcoholic abusers. *Psychological Bulletin,* 815-842, November, 1975.

Lovibond, S.B. and Caddy, G.: Discriminated aversive control in the moderation of alcoholics' drinking behavior. *Behavior Therapy, 1,* 437-444, 1970.

MacAndrew, C. and Edgerton, R.B.: *Drunken Comportment: A Social Explanation.* Chicago, Aldine, 1969.

MacDonald, G. and Bygott, J.: *Impact of Beverage Alcohol on the Criminal Justice system: a Pilot Study.* Toronto, Secretariat for Justice, 1977.

Macinacci, A.: A special type of termporal lobe (psychomotor) seizures following ingestion of alcohol. *Bulletin of the Los Angeles Nuerological Society, 2,* 241-250, 1963.

Madden, P.: *Parole decision making in Ontario.* Toronto, Ministry of Correctional Services, 1980.

Maisto, S. and Cooper, M.: A historical perspective on alcohol and drug treatment outcome research. In Sobell, LC., Sobell, M.B., and Ward, E. (Eds.): *Evaluating Alcohol and Drug Abuse Treatment Effectiveness: Recent Advances.* New York, Pergammon, 1980.

Maisto, S.A. and McCollam, J.B.: The use of multiple measures of life health to assess alcohol treatment outcome: a review and critique. In Sobell, L.C., Sobell, M.B., and Ward, E. (Eds.): *Evaluating Alcohol and Drug Abuse Treatment Effectiveness.* New York, Pergammon, 1980.

Maisto, S.A., Sobell, L.C., and Sobell, M.B.: Comparison of alcoholics' self-report of drinking behavior with reports of collateral informants. *Journal of Consulting and Clinical Psychology,* 1979.

Malfetti, J.L. and Simon, K.J.: Evaluation of a program to rehabilitate drunken drivers. *Traffic Quarterly, 20*(1), 49-59, 1974.

Marlatt, G.A.: Craving for alcohol, loss of control and relapse: a cognitive-behavioral analysis. In Nathan, P.E., Marlatt, G.A., and Loberg, T. (Eds.): *Alcoholism: New Directions in Behavioural Research.* New York, Plenum Press, 1978.

Marlatt, G.A. and Gordon, J.R.: Determinants of relapse: implications for the maintenance of behavioral change. In Davidson, P. and Davidson, S. (Eds.): *Behavioral Medicine: Changing Health Lifestyles.* New York, Brunner/Mazel, 1980.

Martinson, R.: What works? Questions and answers about prison reform. *The Public Interst, 35,* 22-54, 1974.

Martinson, R.: New findings, new views: a note of caution regarding sentencing reform. *Hofstra Law Review, 7*(2), 243-258, 1979.

Maskin, M.B.: The differential impact of work-oriented vs. communication-oriented juvenile correction programs upon recidivism rates in delinquent males. *Jouranl of Clinical Psychology, 32,* 432-433, 1976.

Maultsby, M.C.: *Handbook of Rational Self-Counseling.* Madison, Association for Rational Thinking, 1971.

Maultsby, M.C.: *More Personal Happiness through Rational Self-Counselling.* New York, Institute for Rational Living, 1974.

Maultsby, M.C.: *You and Your Emotions.* Lexington, University of Kentucky Medical Center, 1974.

Mayfield, D.: Alcoholism, alcohol intoxication and assaultive behavior. *Disease of Nervous System, 37,* 288-291, 1976.

McCord, J.: *Correctional Group Counseling: An Evaluation.* Paper presented at the National Conference on Criminal Justice Evaluation, 1977.

McGrath, J., OBrien, J., and Liftik, J.: Coercive treatment for alcoholic "driving under the influence of liquor" offenders. *British Journal of Addiction, 72*(3), 233-229, 1977.

McLachlan, J.F.C.: Benefit from group therapy as a function of patient-therapist match on conceptual level. *Psychotherapy Theory, Research and Practice, 9,* 317-323, 1972.

McLachlan, J.F.C.: Therapy strategies, personality orientation and recovery from alcoholism. *Canadian Psychiatric Association Journal, 19*(1), 25-30, 1974.

McLellan, A.T., Luborsky, L., Woody, G.E., and O'Brien, C.P.: Improved diagnostic evaluation instrument for substance abuse patients. The addiction severity index. *Journal of Nervous and Mental Disease, 168,* 26-33, 1980.

McLellan, A.T., Woody, G.E., Luborsky, L., O'Brien, C.D., and Druley, K.A.: Increased effectiveness of substance abuse treatment: a prospective study of patient-treatment "matching." *Journal of Nervous and Mental Disease, 171,* 597-605, 1983.

Meck, D.S. and Baither, R.: The relation of age to personality adjustment among DWT offenders. *Journal of Clinical Psychology, 36*(1), 342-345, 1980.

Merry, J.: The "loss of control" myth. *Lancet, 1,* 1257-1258, 1966.

Merton, R.K.: *Social Theory and Social Structure.* Glencoe, Free Press, 1957.

Meyer, C.K., Magedanz, T., Kieselhorst, B.C., and Chapman, S.G.: *A Social-Psychological Analysis of Police Assailants.* Norman, Bureau of Government Research, University of Oklahoma, April, 1978.

Miller, P.M.: An analysis of chronic drunkenness offenders with implications for behavioral intervention. *International Journal of the Addictions, 75,* 995-1005, 1975(a).

Miller, P.M.: Behavioral intervention program for chronic public drunkenness offenders. *Archives of General Psychiatry, 32*(7), 915-918, 1975(b).

Miller, P.M.: *Behavioural Treatment of Alcoholism.* New York, Pergamon, 1976.

Miller, W.R.: Behavioral treatment of problem drinkers: a comparative outcome study of three controlled drinking therapies. *Journal of Consulting and Clinical Psychology, 46,* 74-86, 1978.

Miller, W.R., Crawford, V.L. and Taylor, C.A.: Significant others as corroborative source for problem drinkers. *Addictive Behaviors, 4,* 67-70, 1979.

Miller, W.R.: *The Addictive Behaviors, Treatment of Alcoholism, Drug Abuse, Smoking, and Obesity.* New York, Pergamon, 1980.

Miller, P.: Theoretical and Practical Issues in Substance Abuse Assessment and Treatment. In Miller, W.R. (Ed.): *The Addictive Behaviors.* New York, Pergamon, 265-291, 1980.

Moczydlowski, K.: Predictors of success in a correctional halfway house for youthful and adult offenders. *Corrective and Social Psychiatry and Journal of Behavior Technology Methods and Therapy, 26*(2), 59-72, 1980.

Moos, R., Bromet, E., Tsu, V., and Moos, B.: Family characteristics and the outcome of treatment for alcoholism. *Journal of Studies on Alcohol, 40,* 77-78, 1979.

Morris, N. and Hawkins, G. *The Honest Politician's Guide to Crime Control.* Chicago, University of Chicago Press, 1970.

Moskowitz, H. and Depry, D.: The effects of alcohol upon auditory vigilance and divided attention tasks. *Quarterly Journal of Studies on Alcohol, 29,* 54-63, 1968.

Mottin, J.L.: Drug-induced attenuation of alcohol consumption: a review and evaluation of claimed, potential or current therapies. *Quarterly Journal of Studies of Alcohol, 34,* 444-472, 1973.

Moynihan, N.H.: Alcohol and blood sugar. *Alcoholism, 1,* 180-187, 1965.

Mrad, D.F. and Krasnoff, A.G.: Use of MMPI and demographic variables in predicting dropouts from a correctional therapeutic community. *Offender Rehabilitation, 1*(2), 193-201, 1976.

Nathan, P.E.: Alcoholism. In Leitenberg, H. (Ed.): *Handbook of Behaviour Modification.* Englewood Cliffs, Prentice Hall, 1976.

Nathan, P. and Briddel, D.W.: Behavioral assessment and treatment of alcoholism. In Kissin, B. and Begleiter, H. (Eds.): *The Biology of Alcoholism.* New York, Plenum, 1977.

National Institute on Alcohol Abuse and Alcoholism. Program Analysis and Evaluation Branch. *An Overview of Seven NIAAA Alcoholism Treatment Programs,* 1976.

NCCD. National Probation and Parole Institutes, *Uniform Parole Reports Newsletter,* January, 1972.

Nimmer, R.: *Two Million Unnecessary Arrests: Removing a Social Concern from the Criminal Justice System.* Chicago, American Bar Association, 1971.

O'Donnell, C.R., Lydgate, T. and Fo, W.S.: The buddy system: review and follow-up. In Ross, R.R. and Gendreau, P. (Eds.): *Effective Correctional Treatment.* Toronto, Butterworths, 1980.

O'Donnell, J.A., Voss, H.L., Clayton, R.R., Slatin, C.T., and Room, R.G.W.: *Young Men and Drugs — A Nationwide Survey.* Washington, D.C., National Institute for Drug Abuse, 1976.

Ogborne, A.C. and Barnet, A.: Brief report: abstinence and abusive drinking among affiliates of alcoholics anonymous: are these the only alternatives? *Addictive Behaviors,* 189-202, 1982.

Orford, J., Guthrie, S., Nicholls, P., Oppenheimer, E., Egert, S., and Hensman, C.: Self-reported coping behavior of wives of alcoholics and its association with drinking outcome. *Journal of Studies on Alcohol, 36,* 1254-1267, 1975.

Orford, J., Oppenheimer, E., Egert, S., Hensman, C., and Guthrie, S.: The cohesiveness of alcoholism complicated marriages and its influence on treatment outcome. *British Journal of Psychiatry, 128,* 318-339, 1976.

Pallone, N.J. and Tirman, R.J.: Correlate of substance abuse remission in alcoholism rehabilitation: effective treatment of symptom abondonment. *Offender*

Rehabilitation, 3(1), 1978.

Palmer, S.: *The Psychology of Murder.* New York, Corwell, 1962.

Paredes, A., Gregory, D., and Jones, B.M.: Induced drinking and social adjustment in alcoholics: development of a therapeutic model. *Quarterly Journal of Studies on Alcohol, 35,* 1279-1293, 1974.

Paterson, A.S.: Hypnosis as an adjunct to the treatment of alcoholics and drug addicts. *International Journal of Offender Therapy and Comparative Criminology, 18*(1), 40-45, 1974.

Patterson, G.R. andReid, J.B.: Intervention for families of aggressive boys: a replication study. *Behavior Research and Therapy, 11,* 383-394, 1973.

Pattison, E.M., Brissindin, A. and Wohl, T.: Assessing specific effects of inpatient group psychotherapy. *International Journal of Group Psychotherapy, 17,* 283-297, 1967.

Pattison, E.M.: A conceptual approach to alcoholism treatment goals. *Addictive Behaviors, 1,* 177-192, 1976.

Pattison, E.M. (Ed.): *Selection of Treatment for Alcoholics.* New Brunswick, N.J., Journal of Studies on Alcohol, Inc, 1982.

Peele, S.: Through a glass darkly. *Psychology Today,* 38-42, April, 1983.

Pendery, M.L., Maltzman, I.M., and West, L.J.: Controlled drinking by alcoholics? New findings and a revaluation of a major affirmative study. *Science, 217,* 169-174, 1982.

Pernanen, K.: Alcohol and crimes of violence. In Kissin, B. and Begletier, H. (Eds.): *The Biology of Alcoholism, Vol. IV — Social Aspects.* New York, Plenum, 1976.

Pernanen, K.: *Experiences of violence and their association with alcohol use in the general population of a community.* Paper presented at the Annual Meeting of the American Society of Criminology, Philadelphia, November, 1979.

Pernanen, K.: Theoretical aspects of the relationship between alcohol use and crime. In Collins, J.J. (Ed.): *Drinking and Crime: Perspectives on the Relationships between Alcohol Consumptionand Criminal Behavior.* New York, Guilford, 1981.

Petersilia, J.: Which inmates participate in prison treatment programs? *Journal of Offender Counselling Services and Rehabilitation, 4,* 121-135, 1979.

Petersilia, J., Greenwood, P.W., and Lavin, M.: *Criminal Careers of Habitual Felons.* Washington, D.C., U.S. Government Printing Office, 1978.

Phillips, E.L., Phillips, E.E., Fixsen, D., and Wolf, M.: Behavior shaping works for delinquents. *Psychology Today,* 75-76, June, 1973.

Pickens, R., Bigelow, G., and Griffiths, R.: An experimental approach to treating chronic alcoholism: a case study and one year follow-up. *Behavior Research and Therapy, 11,* 321-325, 1973.

Platt, J.J., Perry, G.M., and Metzger, D.S.: The evaluation of a heroin addiction treatment program within a correctional environment. In Ross, R.R. and Gendreau, P. (Eds.): *Effective Correctional Treatment.* Toronto, Butterworths, 1980.

Platt, J.J. and Duome, M.J.: *TIPS: Training in Interpersonal Problem-Solving Skills.* Philadelphia: Hahnemann Medical College, 1981.

Poley, W., Lea, G., and Vine, G.: *Alcoholism: A Treatment Manual.* New York: Gardiner Press, 1979.

Polich, J.M., Armor, D.J., and Braiker, H.B.: *The Course of Alcoholism: Four Years after Treatment.* New York, Wiley, 1981.

Pollack, S.: *Drinking Driver and Traffic Safety: Final Repot.* Los Angeles, University of Sourthern California Public Systems Research Institute, 1973.

Pomerleau, O. and Adkins, D.: Evaluating behavioral and traditional treatment for problem drinkers. In Sobell, L.C., Sobell, M.B., and Ward, E *Evaluating Alcohol and Drug Treatment Effectiveness.* Toronto, Pergamon, 1980.

Pratt, A.D.: A mandatory treatment program for skid row alcoholics; its implication for the uniform and intoxication treatment act. *Journal of Studies on Alcohol, 36,* 166-170, 1975.

Preble, E. and Miller, T.: Methadone, wine and welfare. In Weppner, R.S. (Ed.): *Street Ethnography.* Beverly Hills, Sage, 1977.

President's Commission. *Task Force Report: Drunkenness.* Washington, D.C., U.S. Government Printing Office, 1967.

Rada, R.: Alcoholism and forcible rape. *American Journal of Psychiatry, 132,* 444-446, 1975.

Research Triangle Institute. *Overview: Treatment Outcome Prospective Study* (TOPS). Research Triangle park, N.C., Reserach Triangle Institute, 1980.

Ritson, B.: Personaliy and prognosis in alcoholism. *British Journal of Psychiatry, 118,* 79-82, 1971.

Rix, K.J.B.: *Alcohol and Alcoholism* Montreal, Eden Press, 1977.

Robinson, J. and Smith, G.: The effectiveness of correctional programs. *Crime and Delinquency, 17,* 67-80, 1971.

Roffman, R.A. and Froland, C.: Drug and alcohol dependencies in prisons. *Crime and Delinquency, 22,* 359-366, 1976.

Roizen, J. and Schneberk, D.: In Aarrens, M., Cameron, T., Roizen, J., Roizen, R., Room, R., Schneberk, D., and Wingard, D. (Eds.): *Alcohol, Casualties and Crime.* Berkeley, Social Research Group, 1977.

Romig, D.A.: *Justice for our Children.* Lexington, D.C. Heath, 1978.

Room, R.: Treatment-seeking populations and larger realities. In Edwards, G. and Grant, M.: *Alcoholism Treatment in Transition.* Baltimore, University Park press, 1980.

Rosenblatt, S.M., Gross, M.M., Malenowski, B., Broman, M., and Lewis, E.: Marital status and multiple psychiatric admissions for alcoholism. *Quarterly Journal of Studies on Alcohol, 32,* 1092-1096, 1971.

Roslund, B. and Larson, C.A.: Crimes of violence and alcohol abuse in Sweden. *International Journal of the Addictions, 14*(8), 1103-1115, 1979.

Ross, R.R.: Violence in, violence out: child-abuse and self-mutilation in adolescent offenders. *Canadian Journal of Criminology, 22,* 273-287, 1980.

Ross, R.R.: From therapy to teaching: some reflections on effective correctional programming. *Canada's Mental Health, 30*(4), 1-13, 1982.

Ross, R.R., Currie, C., and Krug-McKay, B.: *The Female Offender: Treatment and Training.* Toronto, Ontario Ministry of Correctioal Sevices, 1980.

Ross, R.R. and Fabiano, E.: *Time to Think Cognition and Crime: Link and Remediation.* Ottawa, Solicitor General, 1981.

Ross, R.R. and Fabiano, E.: *Effective Correctional Treatment: Cognitive Components.* Ottawa, Department of Criminology, 1982.

Ross, R.R. and Fabiano, E.: *The Cognitive Model of Crime and Delinquency Preventioon and Rehabilitation, I: Assessment Procedures.* Toronto, Ontario Ministry of Correctional Services, 1983.

Ross, R.R. and Fabiano, E.: *The Cognitive Model of Crime and Delinquency Preventin and Rehabilitation, II: Intervention Techniques.* Toronto, Ontario Ministry of Correctional Services, 1983.

Ross, R.R. and Fabiano, E.: *Thinking Straight: The Cognitive Model of Crime and Delinquency Prevention and Rehabilitation.* Johnson City, Institute of Social Sciences and Arts, 1985 (in press).

Ross, R.R. and Gendreau, P.: *Effective Correctional Treatment.* Toronto, Butterworths, 1980.

Ross, R.R. and Gendreau, P.: *Offender Change: An Effective Alternative to Incarceration.* Ottawa, Solicitor General, 1983.

Ross, R.R. and McKay, H.B.: A study of institutional treatment programs. *International Journal of Offender Therapy and Comparative Criminology, 20*(2), 167-173, 1976.

Ross, R.R. and McKay, H.B.: Behavioral approaches to treatment in corrections: requiem for a panacea. *Canadian Journal of Criminology, 20*(2), 279-295, 1978.

Roth, L.H. and Rosenberg, N.: Prison adjustment of alcoholic felons. *Quarterly Journal of Studies on Alcohol, 32,* 382-392, 1971.

Rubington, E.: Referral, past treatment contacts, and length of stay in a halfway house: notes on consistency of societal reactions to chronic drunkenness offenders. *Quarterly Journal of Studies on Alcohol, 31,* 659-668, 1970.

Ruggels, Armor, Polich, Mothershead, and Stephen.: *A Follow-Up Study of Clients at Selected Alcoholism Treatment Centers Funded by the NIAA.* Stanford, Stanford Research Institute, 1975.

Sacramento County Detoxification Center. *Evaluation Report.* June, 1973 – March, 1974. Rockville, N.C.J.R.S., 1974.

Sarason, I.G. and Ganzer, V.J.: Modelling and group discussion in the rehabilitation of juvenille delinquents. In Ross, R.R. and Gendreau, P. (Eds.): *Effective Correctional Treatment,* Toronto, Butterworths, 1980.

Saunders, D.N. and Pemberton, L.J.: *Virginia: Diagnosis Referral and Rehabilitation within the Fairfax Alcohol Safety Action Project.* Washington, D.C., Department of Transportation, 1979.

Schur, E.M.: *Radical Non-Intervention: Rethinking the Delinquency Problem.* Englewood, Cliffs, Prentice-Hall, 1973.

Schmidt, W.K. and Burchiel, S.W.: The pharmacology of drug abuse: a novel approach to drug education at San Quentin. *Drug and Alcohol Dependence, 2*(3), 175-183, 1977.

Schramm, C. and Defillippi, R.: Characteristics of successful alcoholism treatment programs for American workers. *British Journal of Addictions, 70,* 271-275, 1975.

Schuckit, M.A.: Charting what has changed. In Edwards, G. and Grant, M. (Eds.): *Alcoholism Treatment in Transition.* Baltimore, University Park Press, 1980.

Scoles, P., and Fine, E.W.: Short-term effects of an educational program for drinking drivers. *Journal of Studies on Alcohol, 38*(3), 633-637, 1977.

Scott, E.M.: Treatment successes with criminals. *International Journal of Offender Therapy and Comparative Criminology, 21*(1), 11-17, 1977.

Scott, E.M.: Group therapy with convicts on work release in Oregon. *International Journal of Offender Therapy and Comparative Criminology, 20*(3), 225-235, 1976.

Scott, E.M., Keener, J., and Manaugh, T.S.: Treatment of alcoholism in an outpatient clinic in Oregon. *International Journal of Offender Therapy and Comparative Criminology, 21,* 141-153, 1977.

Sechrest, L., White, S.O., and Brown, G.D. (Eds.): *The Rehabilitation of Criminal Offenders.* Washington, D.C., National Academy of Sciences, 1979.

Shelton, J., Hollister, L.E. and Gocka, E.F.: The drinking behavior interview: an attempt to quantify alcoholic impairment. *Diseases of the Nervous System, 30,* 464-467, 1969.

Shore, M.F. and Massimo, J.L.: Fifteen years after treatment. A follow-up study of comprehensive vocationally-oriented psychotherapy. In Ross, R.R. and Gendreau, P. (Eds.): *Effective Correctional Treatment.* Toronto, Butterworths, 1980.

Shupe, L.M.: Alcohol and crime. *Journal of Criminal Law, Criminology and Police Science, 44,* 661-664, 1954.

Sielaff, A.: Wisconsin buys map program: bicentennial group cities report. *American Journal of Correction, 39*(4), 18-38, 1977.

Shadel, C.A.: Aversion treatment of alcohol addiction. *Quarterly Journal of Studies on Alcohol, 5,* 216-228, 1944.

Silver, L.B., Dublin, C.C., and Louri R.S.: Does violence breed violence? *American Journal of Psychiatry, 126,* 152-153, 1969.

Skelton, W.D.: Alcohol, violent behavior, and the electroencephalogram. *Southern Medical Journal, 63,* 465-566, 1970.

Skinner, H. Different strokes for different folks: differential treatment for alcohol abuse. In Mayer, Roger E. et al. (Eds.): *Evaluation of the Alcoholic: Implications for Research Theory and Treatment.* Research Monograph #5. Rockville, National Institute on Alcohol Abuse and Alcoholism, 1981.

Smart, R.: Spontaneous recovery in alcoholics: a review and analysis of the available research. *Drug and Alcohol Dependence, 1,* 177-185, 1975.

Smart, R.G., Finney, J.W. and Funston, K.: The effectiveness of post-detoxication referrals: effects on later detoxication admissions, drunkenness and criminality. *Drug and Alcohol Dependence, 2*(3), 149-155, 1977.

Smart, R.G.: Do some alcoholics do better in some types of treatment than others? *Drug and Alcohol Dependence, 3,* 67-75, 1978(b).

Smith, A.B. and Berlin, L.: Can criminals be treated? *New England Journal of*

Prison Law, 3, 487-502, 1977.

Smith, C.G.: Alcoholics: their treatment and their wives. *British Journal of Psychiatry, 115,* 1039-1042, 1969.

Sobell, M.B. and Sobell, L.C.: Individualized behavior therapy for alcoholics. Rationale, procedures, preliminary results and appendix. *California Mental Health Research Monograph No. 13.* Sacramento, 1972.

Sobell, M.B. and Sobell, L.C.: Alcoholics treated by individualized behavior therapy: one year treatment outcome. *Behavior Research and Therapy, 11,* 599-618, November, 1973.

Sobell, L.C. and Sobell, M.B.: Drunkenness: a special circumstance in crimes of violence. *International Journal of Addictions, 10,* 869-882, 1975.

Sobell, M.B. and Sobell, L.C.: Second year treatment outcome of alcoholics treated by individualized behavior therapy: results. *Behavior Research and Therapy, 14,* 195-215, 1976.

Sobell, L.C. and Sobel, M.B.: Convergent validity: an approach to increasing confidence in treatment outcome conclusions with alcohol and drug abusers. In Sobell, L.C., Sobell, M.B., and Ward, E. (Eds.): *Evaluating Alcohol and Drug Treatment Effectiveness.* Toronto, Pergamon, 1980.

Sobell, L.C., Sobell, M.B., and Ward, E. (Eds.): *Evaluating Alcohol and Drug Abuse Treatment Effectiveness.* Toronto, Pergamon, 1980.

Sobell, L.C., Sobell, M.B., and Christleman, W.C.: The myth of "one drink." *Behavior Research and Therapy, 10,* 119-123, 1972.

Stuart, R.: Operant – interpersonal treatment for marital discord. *Journal of Counselling and Clinical Psychology, 33,* 187-196, 1969.

Swenson, P.R. and Clay, T.R.: Effects of short-term rehabilitation on alcohol consumption and drinking related behaviors: an eight month follow-up study of drunken drivers. *International Journal of the Addictions, 15*(6), 821-838, 1980.

Szasz, T.: Psychiatric diversion in the criminal justice system: a critique. In Barnett, R.E. and Hagel, J.: *Assessing the Criminal: Restitution, Retribution and the Legal Process.* Cambridge, Mass., Ballinger, 1977.

Takala, H.: Alkoholstrejkens inverkan pa updagad brottslighet. (The effect of the alcohol strike on reported crime). *Alkoholpolitik, 36,* 14-16, 1973.

Talland, G.A.: Effects of alcohol on performance in continuous attention tasks. *Psychosomatic Medicine, 27*(4), Pt. 2, 595-604, 1966.

Talland, G.A. and Kasschau, R.: Practice and alcohol effects on motor-skill and attention. *Quarterly Journal of Studies on Alcohol, 26,* 393-401, 1965.

Talland, G.A., Mendelson, J.H. and Ryback: Tests of motor skills in experimentally induced chronic intoxication and withdrawal in alcoholics. *Quarterly Journal of Studies on Alcohol,* Supplement #2, 1964.

Tanay, E.: Psychiatric study of homicide. *American Journal of Psychiatry, 125,* 1252-1258, 1969.

Thomas, W.A.: *Alcoholism Program Survey: Federal Prison System.* Washington, D.C., NIAAA, July, 1978.

Tinklenberg, J.R.: Alcohol and violence. In Bourne, P. and Fox, R. (Eds.): *Alco-*

holism: Progress in Research and Treatment. New York: Academic Press, 1973.

Toch, H.: *Violent Men: An Inquiry into the Psychology of Violence.* Chicago, Aldine, 1969.

Towle, Bosley, Borgeson, Gray, Mothershead and Norwood: *Alcoholism Program Monitoring System Development: Evaluation of the ATC Program.* Stanford: Stanford Research Institute, March, 1973.

Trice, H.M. and Roman, P.M.: Sociopsychological predictions of affiliation with alcoholics anonymous. A longitudinal study of "treatment success." *Social Psychiatry, 5,* 51-59, 1970.

Trice, H.M., Roman, P.M., and Belasco, J.A.: Selection for treatment: a predictive evaluation of an alcoholism treatment regime. *International Journal of the Addictions, 4,* 303-317, 1969.

Truax, C.B. and Carkhuff, R.R.: *Toward Effective Counselling and Psychotherapy.* Chicago, Aldine, 1967.

U.S. Department of Justice. Prisoners and alcohol. *Bureau of Justice Statistics Bulletin.* Washington, D.C., 1983.

Van Dijk, W.K. and Van Dijk-Koffeman, A.: A follow-up study of 211 treated male alcoholic addicts. *British Journal of Addictions, 68,* 3-24, 1973.

Vartia, O.K., Forsander, O.A., and Drusius, F.E.: Blood sugar levels in hangover. *Quarterly Journal of Studies on Alcohol, 21,* 597-604, 1960.

Veckler, A. and Solberg, K.: Alcoholics knowledge about alcohol problems. Its relationship to significant attitudes. *Quarterly Journal of Studies of Alcohol, 34,* 509-513, 1971.

Vera Institute of Justice: *Felony Arrests: Their Prosecution and Dispostion in New York City's Courts.* New York, Vera Institute of Justice, 1977.

Voegtlin, W.L. and Lemere, F.: The treatment of alcohol addiction: a review of the literature. *Quarterly Journal of Studies on Alcohol, 2,* 717-798, 1942.

Vogel-Sprott, M.: Coding and vigilance under alcohol. *Quarterly Journal of Studies on Alcohol, 37,* 1581-1592, 1976.

Vogler, R.E., Weissback, T.A., Compton, J.V., and Martin, G.T.: Integrated behavior change techniques for problem drinkers in the community. *Journal of Consulting and Clinical Psychology, 45,* 267-279, 1977.

Vogler, R.E., Weissback, T.A., and Compton, J.V.: Learning techniques for alcohol abuse. *Behavior Research and Therapy, 15,* 31-38, 1977.

Voss, H.L. and Hepburn, J.R.: Patterns in criminal homicide in Chicago. *Journal of Criminal Law, Criminology, and Police Science, 59*(4), 499-508, 1968.

Wade, T.C., Morton, T., Lind, J., and Ferris, N.: A family crisis intervention approach to diversion from the juvenile justice system. *Juvenile Justice, 28*(3), 43-51, 1977.

Wallerstein, R.S.: *Hospital Treatment of Alcoholism: A Comparative Experimental Study.* New York, Basic Books, 1957.

Waller, I.: *Men Released from Prison.* Toronto, University of Toronto Press, 1974.

Walter, B.: *Lafayette City Court Alcohol Rehabilitation Program: A Statistical Evaluation.* Rockville, N.J.C.R.S., 1975.

Walter, T.L. and Mills, C.M.: A behavioral-employment intervention program for reducing juvenile delinquency. In Ross, R.R. and Gendreau, P. (Eds.): *Effective Correctional Treatment.* Toronto, Butterworths, 1980.

Wells, A.: *Alcoholism Detection Treatment and Rehabilitation within the Criminal Justice System.* Washington, NIAAA, 1973.

Winick, C.: The alcoholic offender. In Toch, H. (Ed.): *The Psychology of Crime and Criminal Justice.* New York, Holt, Rinehart and Warton, 1979.

Winship, G.M.: *Antabuse Treatment in Hospital Treatment of Alcoholism: A Comparative Experimental Study.* R.S. Wallerstein (Ed.), Menninger Clinic Monogr. Ser., No. 11. New York, Basic Books, 23-51, 1957.

Wolfgang, M.E.: *Patterns in Criminal Homicide.* Philadelphia, University of Philadelphia, 1958.

Zelhart, P.F.: *The Alberta Impaired Driver Program Final Report, Phase I.* Edmonton, Department of Psychology, University of Alberta, 1973.

Ziegler, R.: Therapeutic program for the alcoholic offender. *Lambola Alpha Epsilon Journal, 39,* 25-29, 1976.

Ziegler, R., Costello, R., and Horvat, G.: Innovative programming in a penitentiary setting: report from a functional unit. *Federal Probation, 40*(2), 44-49, 1976.

Ziegler, R. and Kohutek, K.: A multimodal treatment approach for incarcerted alcoholics. *Journal of Clinical Psychology, 34*(4), 1005-1009, 1978.

NAME INDEX

M

N

O

SUBJECT INDEX